Essential
Greek
Islands

by
ARTHUR EPERON

Arthur Eperon has been a feature writer, foreign
correspondent, travel and news reporter for many
years. Specialising in food, wine and tourism, he has
written several travel books and contributed to a
number of magazines and newspapers. During his
career he has worked with the *Wish You Were Here*
programme and for the *New York Times*.

Produced by AA Publishing

Written by Arthur Eperon
Verified by Robin Gauldie
Peace and Quiet section
by Paul Sterry

Revised fourth edition 1997
Reprinted 1994, 1995
Revised third edition 1994
Reprinted 1993
Revised second edition 1993
First published 1990

Edited, designed and produced
by AA Publishing.
© The Automobile Association
Maps © The Automobile Association

Distributed in the United Kingdom
by AA Publishing, Norfolk House,
Priestley Road, Basingstoke,
Hampshire RG24 9NY.

A CIP catalogue record for this book
is available from the British Library.

ISBN 0 7495 1331 4

The islands of **Crete**, **Corfu** and
Rhodes are not described in this
guide, but are covered by
separate titles in the *Essential*
Series. (See inside front cover for
a full list of *Essential* titles.)

Published by AA Publishing, which is
a trading name of Automobile
Association Developments Limited,
whose registered office is Norfolk
House, Priestley Road, Basingstoke,
Hampshire RG24 9NY.
Registered number 1878835

Colour Origination by: L.C. Repro &
Sons Ltd., Aldermaston, England

Printed by: Printers S.R.L., Trento,
Italy

Front cover picture: *Church on Páros*

English Spellings of Place-names

The visitor to Greece will find
there are several alternatives. In
general, this book uses the
spellings which correspond with
the maps.
However, while a few may be
confusing, most place-names
involve a difference of only a letter
or two, eg Skýros and Skiros, and
can easily be identified.

Contents

This book employs a simple rating system to help choose which places to visit:

 ✓   'top ten'

◆◆◆ do not miss
◆◆   see if you can
◆   worth seeing if you have time

Country Distinguishing Signs
On several maps, international distinguishing signs have been used to indicate the location of the countries which surround the Greek Islands. Thus:

        Ⓖ = Greece   Ⓣ = Turkey

INTRODUCTION

You go to the smaller Greek islands to relax and rejuvenate. You go for sun, for lazing, to enjoy the beauty of the countryside and the sea. If you want organisation and order on holiday, or if you like to plan your sightseeing and evening action to a timetable, you will be very frustrated.

On the big tourist islands of Corfu, Rhodes and Crete (described in other *Essential* guides), you can find international hotels with smooth service and such comforts as efficient lifts and modern bathrooms. Even the buses run on time. On small islands such trappings do not matter, and after a few hours you will not care, either.

You will learn again to take delight in simpler things, like the silver light on the blue sea, sun on white houses with blue doors and shutters, conversation, friendship and the smell of dishes cooking in copper pans on the stove of a taverna. You will delight in the wild flowers which decorate the fields and ditches of farms which know no weedkillers: poppies and many-coloured buttercups, purple Venus's looking-glass, yellow and white crown daisies and

Despite the growing number of visitors, Skópelos remains a quiet and undeveloped island, perfect for a get-away-from-it-all holiday

dozens more flourish prolifically in spring, while wild crocuses and little sweet-scented narcissi bloom in autumn.

You may find yourself passing an hour watching a fishing boat sail across the horizon or a donkey trudging up a hillside, and you will not regard it as time wasted.

Eccentric plumbing turns some people against the Greek Islands. The water may go off for hours during the summer when water becomes precious. The floor of the shower room in your pension may flood to 3 inches before the primitive drain copes. But it will soon dry and so will your feet. Clothes are no problem. You need only be semi-formal to visit a church and you will have little chance to show off your holiday wardrobe. Your jeans or slacks will dry in the sun between breakfast and supper; meantime you can live in your bathing costume and a shirt.

Tourism has changed virtually every Greek island dramatically. Where less than 20 years ago the only contact with the outside world might have been a twice-weekly ferry to the mainland, now holiday jets fly in daily from dozens of European cities. Islanders who started out renting rooms in their homes to visitors now own small hotels and apartment complexes. And gleaming hydrofoils and charter yachts anchor beside wooden fishing boats in island harbours.

Contrary to cherished myth, Greece's smaller isles are more radically affected by the tourism boom than their larger neighbours. They have fewer and smaller beaches and less space for development, and in the summer months their few hundred inhabitants are often well outnumbered by holiday-makers.

But you can still get away from the crowds and find true island solitude. Avoid July and August, or seek out tiny hill villages and remote coves, and you will indeed find the Greece that everybody dreams about. Some islands, such as the Cyclades, can be windy in April when the weather and ferries are unpredictable; May is more settled. June starts to get hot and July and August can be too hot for comfort. September is delightful in most isles and October balmy and pleasant in the more southerly ones, with few other tourists about. But there is no 'best time' to go to the Greek Islands. It is a personal matter.

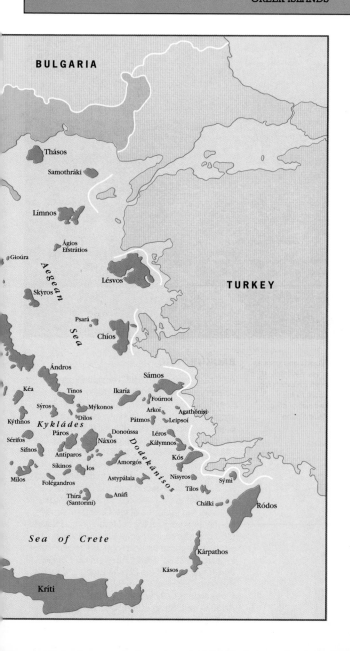

Woods and groves cover Skíathos, even growing right down to the sweeps of clean yellow sand

BACKGROUND

All Greek islands are different in history and scenery. Some are lush and green, others have near-lunar landscapes of volcanic rock. At times neighbouring islands were sworn enemies, and you can still hear old men call people of the next island 'pirates' or 'robbers'. Classical Greece was by no means a united country. It was a series of city-states when the Persians set out to conquer it in the 5th century BC. Some islands sided with the Persians against Athens – a choice they rued after the unexpected victories of the Greeks over the mighty Persian Empire at Marathon and Salamis (480 BC). More isles backed the Spartans against Athens in the fearsome Peloponnesian War from 431 to 404 BC. All eventually came under the sway of the Roman Empire; then the Byzantine Empire. When Byzantium (also called Constantinople, now Istanbul) fell, most of the Aegean and Ionian islands were seized by Venice, others by the Genoese and the Knights of St John. Almost all (except for the Ionian islands) eventually fell to the Turkish Ottoman Empire, which ruled most of Greece from the mid-15th century until 1829, and retained many of the eastern islands until 1912. Some islands remained in Venetian hands much longer: Crete resisted until 1669 and little Tínos until 1718, and relics of the centuries of Venetian rule can be seen on almost every island. The Greeks resented Venetian rule, and frequently sided with the Turks against Venice. In the chaotic centuries before and after the fall of Byzantium, many islands were raided by pirates (Christian and Muslim) who looted their churches and enslaved their people, leaving them deserted. This is why so many island villages are not conveniently located down by the harbour but are perched above it on easily defended hilltops.

Many islands prospered under Ottoman rule, and Greek shipowners and captains controlled most of the sea-trade of the Ottoman Empire, which by the 18th century controlled the whole Eastern Mediterranean. Sými enjoyed tax exemptions because it built and crewed the fast-sailing *skaphes* which the Turks used as

Santoríni is covered with pumice and lava, legacy of countless volcanic eruptions over the centuries; it is not, therefore, a particularly attractive island, but it is most spectacular

BACKGROUND

This elderly couple from Skópelos are typical of the friendly people of the Greek Isles

courier-boats. Chíos received special privileges for producing the *mastika* gum which Turkish ladies loved to chew. The islands of the Saronic Gulf grew wealthy on trade. Nevertheless, it was these island sailors who in 1821 joined westernised expatriate Greeks and guerrilla leaders (*klephts*) from the mainland in the great rising which became the War of Independence. Turkish ships proved no match for Greek fire-ships, and when a combined British, French and Russian fleet, sent to enforce a truce, sank the entire Turkish-Egyptian fleet at Navarino in 1827, Greek victory was certain. The islands of the Cyclades group became part of the new Greek State, which at first included only the southern part of the new Greece. The Ionian islands were ruled by Britain (which had seized them from the French during the Napoleonic Wars). The Northeast Aegean islands remained in Turkish hands until 1912, when they were freed to join Greece. And the Dodecanese were seized from the Turks by Italy in 1912 and did not fly the Greek flag until 1947.

Despite such varying histories, it is surprising that the people of the islands have all kept their essential Greekness and their loyalty to Greece.

One thing the islands have in common to this day, together with their love of the sea, which still rules their lives, is a distrust and awe of Athens, which seems to them to rule and tax them like an absentee landlord.

WHAT TO SEE

SARONIC ISLES

AÍGINA (AEGINA)

Only 40 minutes by hydrofoil, or 1½ hours by ferry, from Piréas, Aígina remains an independent island quite different from Athens. The atmosphere is carefree and happy. Weekend invasions by Athenians, its growing popularity with foreign visitors and cruise passengers making a quick trip to the magnificent temple of Aphaia, have changed it, but not fundamentally. Fishing and agriculture are still more important than tourism, though fish scarcities are beginning to hurt. Growing pistachio nuts is particularly lucrative. They are harvested in August. Aígina is pronounced 'Ayina', with the stress on the first 'A'.

◆◆
AÍGINA TOWN

The town is proud to have been, in 1826, the first capital of Free Greece during the fight for independence against the Turks. The first president, Capodistria, set up the Greek government here. The first free newspaper was published, the first drachma minted carrying a phoenix head to show Greece risen from the ashes. The austere pink tower of Markellos was the first building of Free Greece. What is now the public library was the Residence of the president, who worked and slept upstairs while drachma were minted below. Capodistria moved to Nauplion in the Peloponnese in 1829 because the Allied fleet was there. He was murdered by Greek political opponents. Aígina now has a busy main harbour (a present from an American, Samuel Greenly Howe) and a fishing harbour lined with coloured boats and a tiny quayside fishermen's chapel of Ágios Nikólaos, patron saint of sailors. Fishermen catch a lot of *marides* (whitebait). You can step across the gangplanks of boats to buy your vegetables, fruit and fish, laid out as if in a shop. There are few tourist, souvenir or clothes shops for foreigners. Shops, bars and restaurants are mostly aimed at locals or Athenians. Only one column survives of Apollo's Temple on Kolona hill, but there is an archaeological museum (*open*: Tuesday to Saturday 08.30–15.00hrs; Sunday 10.00–15.00hrs; *closed*: Monday). A walk northwards takes you to Livadi, where a plaque marks the whitewashed house where the Cretan Nikos Kazantzakis wrote *Zorba the Greek*.

The 5th-century BC Temple of Aphaia on Aígina is one of the most beautiful classical temples in Greece

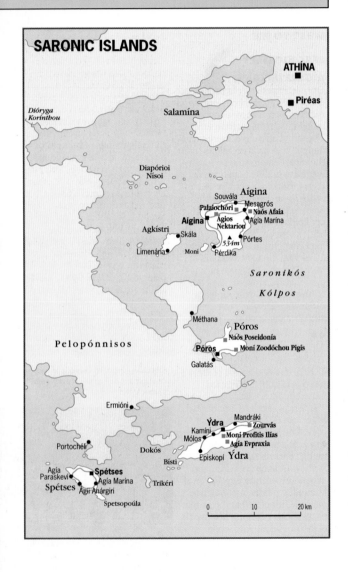

SARONIC ISLANDS

ATHÍNA

Piréas

Dióryga Korínthou

Salamína

Diapórioi Nísoi

Souvála   Aígina
                        Mesagrós
Palaióchóri   Naós Afaía
Aígina   Ágios   Agía Marína
              Nektárion
Agkístri   Skála   Pórtes
                        ▲534m
Limenária   Moní   Pórtes
                  Pérdika

Saronikós

Kólpos

Méthana   Póros
              Naós Poseidonía
        Póros   Moní Zoodóchou Pigís
Galatás

Pelopónnisos

Ermióni
                  Mandráki
              Ýdra   Zourvás
        Karníni   Moní Profítis Ilías
        Mólos   Agía Evpraxía
Portochéli
        Dokós   Ýdra
              Bísti   Episkopí
Agía
Paraskeví   Spétses
        Agía Marína
Spétses   Ágir Anárgiri   Trikéri
        Spetsopoúla

0   10   20 km

The colourful fishing harbour in Aígina Town

◆◆◆
PÉRDIKA (PÉRDHIKA)

Five and a half miles (9km) south from Aígina Town, Pérdika is a charming fishing village with a line of good fish restaurants, where you choose your fish then drink your wine on the white terrace above the fishing boats while the fish are grilled over charcoal.

◆◆
MONÍ

From Pérdika you can see the delightful little island of Moní, seemingly a stone's throw away. Named because it used to belong to a monastery, it now belongs to the Touring Club of Greece and you pay a small entrance fee on your boat fare. There is a campsite in summer, beautifully clear water, a small beach, footpaths through woods, then rocky scrub pungent with wild herbs, especially sage (which is made into tea as a blood purifier). Wild flowers bloom from spring until September. Peacocks may join you on the beach, and hiding in the hills are splendid but shy wild kri-kri goats with great long horns. Boats from Pérdika take 10 minutes to Moní.

◆
HELLANION

Inland towards Pórtes is Hellanion, 11 miles (18km) from Aígina Town, where Aikos, son of Aígina, prayed to Zeus for rain during a drought all over Greece. Zeus granted his request – not surprisingly, for Zeus was his father. (Aígina was one of the hundreds of mistresses of the aptly-named Father of the Gods.)

◆
SOUVÁLA

A delightful little port and spa for treating rheumatism and skin diseases. Here you can get away from the intense summer heat.

Ferries call direct from Piréas. You can eat and drink in the evening at harbourside tavernas while you watch the fishing boats go out. Souvála is northeast of Aígina Town, and the road to it passes Kípseli, where there are views to the port from the taverna. Kípseli (meaning 'beehive') was called Halasmeni (ruined) after the ruins of a church – until local girls complained!

◆◆
AGÍA MARÍNA

Agía Marína, on the east coast, 8½ miles (14km) from Aígina Town is the tourist resort of Aígina, built up recently and a little too fast from a seaside village. It is a superb place for children, for sands stretch a long way round the almost landlocked bay and the water is shallow and safe. There are pedalos for hire. Tavernas and restaurants with tables under umbrellas line the sands. There are pensions, small self-catering blocks and small hotels, including the comfortable Apollo set on high rocks. Even its swimming pool has a fine view. Small boats bring cruise passengers ashore. They are herded into coaches and taken up the hill to see Naós Afaía (Temple of Aphaia), then they shop for souvenirs in Agía Marína and are gone within two hours.

Four miles (6.5km) along and just south of the road from Aígina to Agía Marína is the monastery of Ágios Nektaríou, named after a bishop of Aígina who was canonised in 1961, the most recent Greek Orthodox Church saint. The original chapel is reserved for women. The saint's remains are in a new chapel. Twenty-two nuns live in the monastery. Opposite the monastery set on a low hill are the ruins of the former Byzantine and medieval capital Palaiochóri (Palaiokhora), founded in the 9th century AD after a very bloody Arab pirate attack on Aígina Town. But in 1537 the pirate-admiral Barbarossa took Palaiochóri, massacred the men and took away 6,000 women and children as slaves. With Independence in 1826, the people moved back to the coast, dismantling much of their hill capital to build the new one. There were originally 365 13th-century churches in Palaiochóri; only 28 have survived.

◆◆◆
NAÓS AFAÍA (TEMPLE OF APHAIA)

The temple, built in impressive Doric style, stands in a superb position on a wooded ridge with sea views on two sides. One of the most beautiful and complete classical temples in Greece, it was built between 480 and 410 BC and its lovely columns, narrowing from the base to the capital, are much like those of the Parthenon. Twenty-five of the original 32 columns are still there. Alas, the splendid pediment statues were sold in 1811, by the German and British archaeologists who dug them up, to the eccentric King Ludwig of Bavaria. They are now in the Glyptothek Museum in Munich. The temple was dedicated to Aphaia, a goddess little known outside Aígina. She was either a moon goddess or a Cretan Minoan goddess of wisdom and light. The temple is 9 miles (14km) east of Aígina Town, on a hill above Agía Marína.

Accommodation

There are plenty of hotels especially at Agía Marína. Most of those in Aígina Town are old. **The Hotel Brown**, 3 Toti Hatzi, is friendly, C-class (tel: 0297-22271); the **Danae** is B-class (tel: 0297-22424). **Eginitiko Archontiko**, A-class (tel: 0297-24968), in a fine old shopowner's mansion, is one of the new breed of comfortable hotels in restored traditional buildings.

Restaurants (Aígina)

The restaurants and tavernas on the island serve above-average meals. Fish can be outstanding, especially at Pérdika. **Costas**, just outside Agía Marína serves good Greek dishes.

General Information

Population: 11,500
Area: 32sq miles (83sq km)
17 nautical miles from Piréas.
Tourist Office & Tourist Police:
tel: 0297-22391/23333.
Harbour Police: tel: 0297-22328.

How to Get There

Ferries: there are about 10 daily from Piréas, mostly going to Aígina Town, but some call at Agía Marína and Souvála in summer (1½ hrs).
Hydrofoil: from Piréas, every hour in summer (40 mins); fewer in winter. Summer cruise ships make the round trip from Piréas to Aígina, Póros, Ýdra and Spétses. Boat trips can be made from the island to Ýdra and Póros.

PÓROS

Póros consists of two islands connected by a bridge. Its capital, Póros Town, on the smaller island, is so close to Galatás on the Peloponnese mainland that Henry Miller, in *The Colossus of Maroussi*, compared his arrival to sailing through the streets of Venice. The strait is only 280 yards (256m) wide. Sea taxis called *benzina* pop across constantly.

PÓROS TOWN

As you approach, you see two uneven humps with dark green lemon groves; then, as you sail through a narrow, almost secretive entrance into an open bay, the houses of Póros Town

Churches – these are church roof tiles – and houses jostle together busily in Póros Town

appear, like white cubes piled up the sides of a cone. The town has a happy atmosphere. One reason is that the harbour-quay is a market, with stalls selling vegetables, fruit and fish as well as souvenirs and clothes. The stalls share the space with the tables and chairs of bars.
The hump (called Sferia) on which Póros port is sited is small enough to walk round in an hour. A causeway leads to the bigger hump (Kalavria) which is greener, with several coves of shingle shaded by pine. It has a short stretch of tarmac road leading in 2 miles (3km) to Askeli bay in the south, where most of the tourist hotels are. Overlooking the bay is the attractive 18th-century Moní Zoodóchou Pigís (Monastery of the Source of Life).

♦
NAÓS POSEIDÓNIA (TEMPLE OF POSEIDON)
Only a few stone walls remain of the great temple of Poseidon, 9 miles (14km) north of Póros Town, built in 500 BC and once as magnificent as the Aígina temple. In the 18th century its marble blocks were looted, cut into sizes mules could carry, taken to the shore and shipped to Ýdra to build a monastery. The temple was a sanctuary: any fugitive or shipwreck victim was safe within its walls.
Póros makes its living from fishing, tourism and, especially, growing lemons, olives and flowers. Visitors wonder where they grow all these crops until they discover that many farmers also have land across the Galatás straits on the mainland, 5 minutes

by boat. Here is Lemonodassos (the Lemon Forest), with 30,000 lemon trees.

Accommodation
There are two recommended hotels in Póros Town: the **Hotel Póros**, B-class (tel: 0298-22216/8), has great sweeping views; **Dionyssos**, B-class, (tel: 0298-23511/24503), is good value in a pleasant old building.

Restaurants
The **Lagoudera** restaurant on Póros waterfront is one of the best on these islands, serving superb (if pricey) fish.

General Information
Population: 4,000
Area: 9sq miles (23sq km)
31 nautical miles from Piréas.
Tourist Office & Tourist Police: tel: 0298-22256 or 22462.
Harbour Police tel: 0298-22274.

How to Get There
Ferries: the car ferry from Piréas, Aígina and Methana (on the mainland) calls at Póros three times a day (3¾ hours); it continues to Ýdra. There are regular ferries from the island to Galatás on the mainland.
Hydrofoil: every 1 or 2 hours from Zea Marina, Piréas (1hr).

ÝDRA (HYDRA)
Though most visitors stay on Ýdra only a few hours, it has devoted fans and has been called 'the Greek St Tropez'. At first sight this is surprising, for it is bare and rocky, with no good beaches and is often short of water. Cars are banned. You must walk or cycle in the hot sun to see anything outside the port. It is desperately short of

Bird's-eye view of the harbour at
Ýdra, one of the loveliest of the Isles

accommodation because local
laws forbid the building of those
square concrete boxes which
spoil some Greek villages, and,
without a reservation, you will
not find a room in mid-summer.
Old cottages and farms have
been repaired for holiday homes.
The heavy, stone Venetian-style
mansions with beautiful
Italianate interiors have been
restored strictly to their original
style. The port is particularly
photogenic and cosmopolitan. In
mid-summer Ýdra is crowded
and very hot at midday. May
and September are delightful.
Most of the splendid old villas

are private houses. They were
built by shipowners, for Hydriots
were skilled sailors. A few
houses can be visited. Genuine
professional artists are
especially welcome at the old
house of the Tombazis family,
now a School of Fine Art. The
Tsamados house is now a
Merchant Marine School (with
a bar – To Laikon – open to the
public. Ask at the door if you
can see round both of these.
One or two owners open their
villas at times on application.
Ask at the Town Hall.
A long walk of about 1½ hours
by lanes and paths leads to the
monastery of Profitis Elías (Moní
Profitis Ilías) and Convent of
Agía Evpraxia.

Bare and rocky, Ýdra is still a working fishing island

The monastery was founded by refugees from Mount Athos in 1770 and no woman may enter. A few nuns still weave and embroider at the convent and you can buy their work (mostly shawls). You can hire a mule to get here but it is pricey and uncomfortable. There are lovely views.

◆
KAMÍNI
Just over a mile (2km) south of the port is Kamíni, with a small harbour, tavernas and shops. You can swim off the rocks here. Further down this coast is Mólos, where there is a cove for swimming beside a pine forest.

Accommodation
The A-class **Miranda** (tel: 0298-52230), is one of the best small luxury hotels in Greece. The **Ýdra** at 8 Voulgari, (tel: 0298-52102) is in a fine sea-captain's mansion.

Restaurants
Restaurants on the portside are pricey and good fun. The **Three Brothers** restaurant near the cathedral is cheaper and offers very good Greek dishes.

General Information
Population: 2,750
Area: 19⅓sq miles (50sq km)
38 nautical miles from Piréas.
Tourist Office & Tourist Police: Navarchou N Botsi Street (tel: 0298-52205 – season only).
Harbour Police: tel: 0298-52279.

How to Get There
Ferries: There is one ferry daily from Piréas (4hrs 10 mins). Some call at Aígina, Methana (on the mainland) and Póros. Regular boats sail to Ermoní on mainland (⅓hr).
Hydrofoil: 5 times a day from Piréas (Zea Marina), calling at Aígina and Póros (1½hrs).

SPÉTSES (SPETSES)
You can walk round this charming isle in a day. Two-thirds of it is covered in pines and all around the coast are little coves you must reach finally on foot or by sea. No cars are allowed but there are two taxis and one bus, and a partly-tarmac road around the isle resounds to the clomp of horses' hoofs. Horse-drawn fiacres are the main transport. You can hire bicycles, too. Spétses has been a holiday isle

for Athenians since the grand old Possidonion Hotel was built in 1914. It is still open. With a casino operating between the World Wars, it was *the* resort of Greece until the 1960s.

♦♦♦
SPÉTSES TOWN

The capital and port (officially called Spétses but known locally as Dapia after the square near the harbour) spreads for 1¾ miles (3km) along the coast. The Dapia, sprinkled with old cannons, is particularly lively, with fashionable restaurants and bars brightly lit at night. The cheaper bars and tavernas are around the fish market. Old family mansions include the home of the powerful ship-owning Mexis family, now a museum. Built in 1795, the house, half Venetian, half Moorish in style, was like a fortress surrounded by high walls – not for privacy but defence against rival rich shipping families. In the museum itself, among 19th-century local paintings and costumes, is the 'Freedom or Death' flag of the War of Independence, and a casket with the remains of the local Independence heroine Lascarina Bouboulina – a most bellicose admiral. A rich widow with nine children, she continued her father's businesses of making ships and of piracy against Turkish allies. In the Revolution, dressed in the striped costume of Spétses and carrying a cutlass, she led her ships in big naval engagements, often landing to lead her forces. Narrow, cobbled alleyways in the town are inlaid with mythical

marine figures made from coloured pebbles.

By the old harbour (now used by yachts) and the town beach, is a memorial marking the naval battle of 8 September 1822, when Spetsiot brigs and fireships repelled a superior Turkish force. On the nearest weekend to 8 September the scene is re-enacted each year in a regatta with fireworks replacing gunfire. Beside the harbour are large white houses and the cathedral of Ágios Nikólaos, once a monastery. On its clock tower the flag of freedom was first raised in 1821.

♦
ÁGII ANÁRGIRI

Of the many coves along the jagged coastline, the most developed is the shady Ágii Anárgiri, where a village has built up around holiday homes, with a good taverna. Small boats call, the bus stops in summer, or you can walk to it round the road – about 9 miles (15km) – or on island paths. High on a point between here and the little beach of Agía Paraskeví is the large Villa Yasemia (Jasmine), known as the 'House of Magus'. To readers of John Fowles' novel *The Magus*, it is 'Bourani'. Fowles taught at the imposing Anarygirios and Korgialenios School 1¼ miles (2km) west of Spétses Town, founded in 1927 on the model of an English public school.

♦
AGÍA MARÍNA

The beach here, a mile (2km) south from the old harbour, is very popular in summer.

◆
VRELLO
The lovely Vrello valley at the northeast tip of the island, 3¾ miles (6km) from the harbour, is the beauty spot of Spétses.

Accommodation
The old **Possidonion** (tel: 0298-72308) is A-class. **Kasteli**, also class A, has hotel rooms and bungalows (tel: 0298-72311). The B-class **Villa Christina** (tel: 0298-72218), has 12 lovely rooms in a restored 18th-century house. Hotels are booked well in advance. You may have to settle for a room in a private house. There is no campsite.

Restaurants
The food is better than on most isles, and dearer. Speciality is sea bream in a spicy sauce (*psari Spetsiotiko*). **Mandalena's** restaurant on the new harbour waterfront serves good seafood.

General Information
Population: 3,750
Area: 8½sq miles (22sq km)
53 nautical miles from Piréas.
Tourist Office & Tourist Police: Botsari Street (tel: 0298-73100).
Harbour Police: tel: 0298-72245.

How to Get There
Ferries: One daily from Piréas (almost 5½hrs). There are frequent boats to Kosta Ermioni and Porto Heli on the mainland, and one goes daily to Nauplion.
Hydrofoil: regular service from Zea Marina, Piréas (2hrs).

On the wooded isle of Spétses, trees sometimes grow down to the beach

CYCLADES

ÁNDROS

A big mountainous island, wooded, well watered with many olives and vines, Ándros seems better-organised and more prosperous than the other Cyclades Islands, and has fairly few foreign tourists.

It is reached easily from Athens, so it has become a hideaway for well-heeled Athenians. Ironic, for Ándros sided through history with the enemies of Athens, even with the Persians at Salamis. Boats leave the mainland from the scruffy port of Rafina, less than an hour by car or bus from Athens, and land you at the port of Gávrio, which is a bad advertisement for Ándros. It has a big lorry park, uninviting-looking cafés and a temporary look. But a short bus journey soon shows you the island's scenic attraction and undeveloped coastline.

◆◆
BATSÍ

Most foreign visitors stay at the one resort which is slightly developed, Batsí, on a bus route 5 miles (8km) from Gávrio. The easiest place to find a bed, it is in a sheltered bay, with a fishing harbour at one end and a grass-covered sand dune with a beach at the other. A beach with some trees for shade joins them, backed at the harbour end by old-style shops, including one of those very-Greek general stores serving everything from food and wine to books, brooms and nails. There are lively tavernas on the dockside with tables under vines, all specialising in

fish. And there are two banks. A few small hotels round the bay bring you to three small, two-storey apartment blocks. The village is backed by tiers of red-roofed houses reached by steps and terraced farms.

◆◆
ÁNDROS TOWN

Buses continue from Batsí past the ancient capital, Palaiopóli, of which some walls remain, to the capital and port Ándros Town on the east coast. It is a working town still involved in shipping, and is pleasant and interesting. It is built mostly on a finger of land above two good sandy beaches, with remains of a Venetian castle on the end, several museums, and puzzling changes of level.

The main street with old mansions and marble paving is for pedestrians. It leads to a charming little square, Kairis, where you can admire good sea views while taking a drink or a meal, outside or in. Steniés, 3 miles (5km) from the town, has a good beach.

A right branch of the road from Batsí to Ándros leads over Mount Gerakonos to the fishing port of Órmos Korthíou, 18½ miles (30km) from Batsí. It has a small C-class hotel, Korthíou, rooms and restaurants in lanes off the main street. On the road here you pass Palaiokastro, a nice old village with ruins of another Venetian fort.

The road north from Gávrio turns into a track which leads to mountain villages, including attractive Amólochos. A surfaced road leads to the Tower of Ágios Petros, dating

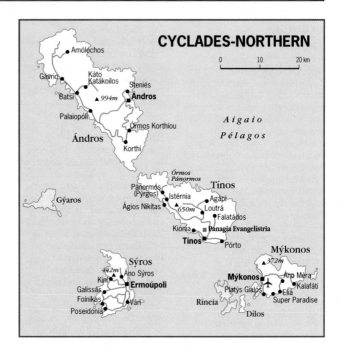

CYCLADES-NORTHERN

from the Hellenistic period –
65 feet (20m) high, its upper
storeys are reached by a
ladder. No one knows whether
it was for storing food, a fort or
a signalling tower. Three miles
(5km) above Batsí is the village
of Káto Katákoilos, with a stream
running through it, three lively
tavernas with music and
exuberant dancing in season.

Accommodation
Ándros: **Hotel Paradissos** is
elegant, old-style and B-class
(tel: 0282-22187). **Aegli**
up some steps off the high street is
C-class (tel: 0282-22303).
Gávrio: **Gávrio Beach Hotel** is
good for C-class (tel: 282-
71312), as is **Korthíou** (tel:
0282-61218) in Korthíou.

Restaurants
The best restaurants are near
the beach in Ándros Town and
near the harbour at Batsí, where
the very best is **Yiannis'**
taverna, below the steps on the
esplanade. Yiannis has a farm
and serves good meat from it.
The **Lykion** in Batsí serves good
value dishes and is pleasant.

General Information
Population: 9,500
Area: 144sq miles (373sq km)
89 nautical miles from Piréas.
Tourist Office: tel: 0282-71250.
Tourist Police: in Gávrio police
station (tel: 028-71220).

How to Get There
Ferries: There is no direct ferry
from Piréas. Take a bus from

Athens to Rafina (55mins) then a ferry to Ándros (2½hrs). Some Rafina ferries call at Tínos and Sýros, others call at Tínos and Mýkonos. There are daily ferries from Ándros to Tínos (2hrs).

TÍNOS

A holy island to modern Greeks, Tínos has been called the 'Orthodox Lourdes'. Pilgrims arrive on the Feast Days of the Virgin: 25 March (The Annunciation) and 15 August (the Assumption).

◆◆
TÍNOS TOWN

The pilgrimage centre in Tínos Town is the neo-classical Church of Panagía Evangelístria (Annunciation), which is hung with hundreds of votive offerings and lamps in silver and even gold, given in thanks by the faithful who still flock here to seek spiritual comfort, relief from afflictions and, perhaps, a miracle cure. During the weeks of the Feasts people queue to kiss the ikon, now decked in gold, diamonds and pearls.

In July 1822, an 80-year-old nun from a local convent, Sister Panagía (now a saint), dreamed that the Virgin revealed to her where an icon could be found in a field. Excavations found the treasure near a ruined church, so the new church was built there. The icon was discovered just as the Greek fight for freedom from the Turks had begun, so it was hailed as a sign from God and the church is a national shrine.

The crypt of the original ruined church, now a chapel, has a spring believed to have curative powers. In a mausoleum alongside are the victims of the cruiser *Elli*. When the festival was at its height on 15 August 1940, an Italian submarine sneaked into Tínos harbour and sank the cruiser, although the two countries were not at war. The sinking vitalised Greek resistance, and infuriated the powerful Greek lobby in the US (who still had not entered World War II).

Tínos Town is rich in museums, including a painting gallery with works of the Ionian School and a Rubens. The archaeological museum (*open*: 08.30–15.00hrs; *closed*: Mondays) includes finds from the Sanctuary of Poseidon and Amphitrite, 2½ miles (4km) northwest of the town at Kiónia, which also has two beaches.

In pilgrimage weeks a great many candles are lit in the revered church in Tínos Town

CYCLADES

Less crowded beaches near the town are at Ágios Sostis, 4½ miles (7km) away, a sweeping sandy beach, and Pórto, 5 miles (8km) away, with new low-built apartments, but no taverna yet. A bus goes from the town pier to the large 12th-century Kechrovounio Convent where the sister had her dream; her embalmed head is here.

◆◆
WEST COAST

The island's west coast has steep tracks to the sea, and gritty beaches. A mountainous main road leads to Órmos Pánormos (Pýrgos locally), 20½ miles (33km) from Tínos Town, where artists work in green marble. There is a museum, a school of fine art and an attractive square with shops selling students' work. This is the green part of the island. From picturesque Istérnia just south, a steep paved road leads to Ágios Nikítas beach – pebbly with a shady cove. This consists of a big old quay, a hotel, some tavernas, rooms and tranquillity.

Accommodation

Tinion, 1 C Alavanou (tel: 0283-22261), B-class, is one of the oldest hotels and is still pleasant and friendly. **Poseidonion**, 4 Paralias (tel: 0283-23123) along the Esplanade, over a good restaurant, is above C-class average, and most of its rooms have wc and shower. **Eleana**, Paralias (tel: 0283-22561), beside Ágios Ioannon Church, is above average for D-class.

Restaurants

Because of the festivals, Tínos Town has plenty of restaurants, tavernas and hotels, **Michalis Taverna**, Gavou Street, is one of the best places to eat.

General Information

Population: 7,700
Area: 75sq miles (195sq km)
86 nautical miles from Piréas.
Tourist Office: tel: 0283-23513.
Tourist Police: tel: 0283-22255.

How to Get There

Ferries: Once or twice a day from Piréas (via Sýros, 4¾hrs) and from Rafina on the mainland (via Ándros, 4hrs). There are also frequent services from Ándros and Mýkonos; less frequent from Sýros. Summer ferries go to Páros and Náxos.

MÝKONOS

Mýkonos is still the most fashionable island in Greece, where Athenians love to own a house. It is rocky and windy, though pretty, with delicate windmills, 365 churches built as votive offerings to heaven, and a lot of beaches.
There is night life of most sorts and the isle is great fun for a few days and nights. Shops in the alleys of the old port sell overpriced jewellery, gold and furs, and, like the streets, get very crowded when cruise passengers arrive. The fashionable beaches are still Paradise, Platys Gialós and Super Paradise, which is unofficially nudist and beloved by gays, though Mýkonos is no longer the gay Mecca of the 1960s and '70s. Less crowded beaches are at Eliá, Anna Bay and the two coves between Paradise and Gialós. The best

Mýkonos is a fashionable place, where a lot of sitting and watching-of-the-world goes on

way to reach beaches in summer is by caique from the harbour. Pick your beach according to the wind. The centre of the isle is rock and gets very hot in summer.

◆◆◆
CHÓRA (MÝKONOS TOWN)

The Chóra, the photogenic port and capital, is well whitewashed, neat and gleaming, and is most alluring, particularly the Alefkandhra ('Little Venice') area. The Archaeological Museum has interesting unusual vases, and funeral jewellery and headstones from the 1st and 2nd centuries BC, taken from Rineia island where the old and sick from the nearby isle of Dílos were sent to die.

◆◆◆
DÍLOS (DELOS)

An earlier generation of tourists used Mýkonos simply as a base to see the archaeological sites on Dílos, the island sanctuary dedicated to Apollo and once as important as Delphi. French archaeologists have excavated the site since 1872 and have done a good job of reconstruction of what is left. Boats leave daily from Mýkonos at about 08.30–09.00hrs returning at 12.30hrs (½ hr trip).

Accommodation

Hotels and restaurants are dearer and smarter than on many other isles and food is often good. Passengers landing by ferry are almost persecuted by touts offering rooms. They will whisk away your luggage, then put you on a bus to where the room is. For those seeking action both day and night,

Windmill and cruise ship, evening light, Mýkonos

Mýkonos port is the place to stay, but rooms there are dearer and scarcer. The **Leto**, with a wonderful harbour view, is best, most fashionable and dearest (tel: 0289-22207). **Philippi**, 32 Kalogera Street (tel:(0289-22294), though D-class, is charming. D-class **Platýs Gialós Beach Hotel** (tel: 0289-22913) is better and dearer than its class suggests. On Ornos Beach, 2 miles (3.5km) from Mýkonos Town, is the convenient **Ornos Beach**, B-class (tel: 0289-22243).

Restaurants
There is a big choice of tavernas and restaurants in the port and Chóra. **Taverna Nikos** (behind the town hall) has a good choice, including roasts. **El Greco's**, on Odos Enoplon Dinameon, is good, but rather pricey; it is a picturesque area at night. At Alefkandhra ('Little Venice'), the **Pelican** restaurant is beautifully placed, and serves good meals.

General Information
Population: 5,500 (very variable as Athenians come and go)
Area: 33sq miles (85sq km)
94 nautical miles from Piréas.
Tourist Office & Tourist Police: on quay (tel: 0289-22482).
Harbour Police: ferry end of harbour, post office building (tel: 0289-22218).

How to Get There
Air: Charters direct from Europe. Flights from Athens (50mins), 7–11 a day; Irakleío (Crete), daily (1hr 10mins); Rhodes, daily (2hrs); Santoríni, daily (1hr 40mins). There is a service to Kós in summer.
Ferries: Daily from Piréas (via Sýros and Tínos, 5½hrs), and from Rafina (via Ándros and Tínos or Sýros, 5hrs). Also direct from Sýros (2hrs), Tínos (1hr) and Náxos. Daily in summer to Páros, Íos and Santoríni. High summer express catamaran to Santoríni, Sýros and Irakleío.
Caique: Daily to Dílos, weather permitting (½ hr).

SÝROS
Called locally 'The Rock', Sýros is mostly dry and barren, with few roads in the north, but there are hills with some greenery and beaches in the south.

◆
ERMOÚPOLI
Before the Corinth canal was cut, Ermoúpoli was the most important port in Greece. Then Piréas replaced it. But it is still centre for many Cyclades ferry routes. Passengers change ferries, often staying overnight,

so there are hotels, rooms, tavernas and some good restaurants. Its shipyards keep busy, it makes many of those 'Greek' cotton shirts and dresses which tourists love, has tanneries and iron foundries. And it makes *loukoumia* (Turkish – or Greek – Delight) in many colours and flavours. In its heyday, Ermoúpoli was an elegant town. Architects from France, Italy and Germany designed houses with wrought-iron balconies, fine churches, public buildings and big villas for shipowners and merchants. Its greatest splendour was the Apollo Municipal Theatre, a copy of La Scala in Milan. Until early this century, it presented an opera festival by a company from Italy. Now it is derelict. Many houses are shut because of Greek inheritance laws and family arguments. Plateia Miaoulis, the marble-paved main square, is 19th-century neo-classic with a sad faded charm, but brightens up with the evening *voltá* when everyone walks around for hours.

ÁNO SÝROS
Well worth seeing is the medieval Venetian Roman Catholic town, Áno Sýros, high above the port. You can walk up the stepped streets and alleys, which takes a rewarding 45 minutes, or go round the 1¼ miles (2km) by taxi. Winding, steep narrow streets criss-cross among many chapels and a Jesuit Convent founded by Louis XIII of France. In the hilltop square is St George's Cathedral and the bishop's palace.

The small resort of Foínikas on the west coast has some hotels. Vári in the south is another resort with hotels and tavernas. Bus services are good.

Accommodation
Ermoúpoli has plenty of choice of hotels. Smartest is the A-class **Ypatia** (tel: 0281-23575). **Vourlis**, 5 Mavrogordatou, (tel: 0281-28440) on the east cliff, also A-class, is in a 19th-century villa. **Cyclades**, E-class, (tel: 0281-42255), offers cheap accommodation at Foínikas.

Restaurants
Eat round Ermoúpoli's main square and watch the *voltá*.

General Information
Population: 19,500
Area: 33sq miles (86sq km)
83 nautical miles from Piréas.
Tourist Office: tel: 0281-26725 or 22375.
Police: just off Plateia Miaoulis (tel: 0281-22610). Harbour Police: (tel: 0281-22690).

How to Get There
Ferries: Daily sailings from Piréas (4¼hrs), and on to Tínos (1hr) and Mýkonos (2hrs). The Mýkonos route is useful, as there are daily sailings from there to Tínos, Ándros and Rafina (on the mainland, 5hrs); on Sundays the ferry calls in at Sýros (3½hrs to Rafina). Less frequent boats go to Náxos, Íos, Santoríni, Síkinos, Folégandros, Mílos, Sífnos, Sérifos, Kýthnos, Ikaría, Sámos, Irakleío (Crete), Amorgós, Donoússa and Astypálaia. There are also seasonal small ferry boats to various islands, and an express catamaran between Santoríni and Crete calls in mid-summer.

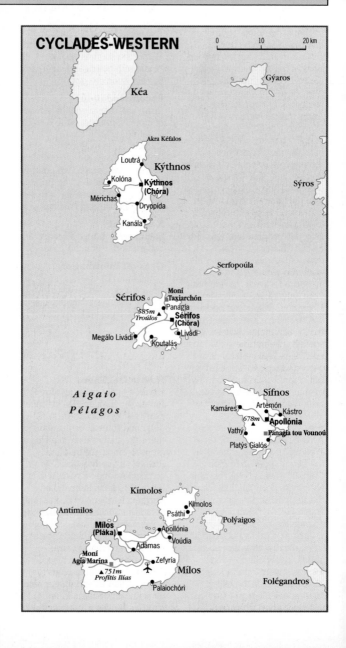

Sífnos is a walker's island, especially if you want to go to this dramatically sited church

SÍFNOS

An enchanting island, which has the appearance of an arid mountain as you catch approach it, Sífnos hides its fertile valleys and carefully cultivated terraced fields a short bus ride inland from the lively little port of Kamáres.

◆
KAMÁRES

Here the ferries come in, yachts come and go, and fishing boats unload their catch and sell it on the quayside, weighing the lobsters as the taverna owners take their pick. The tavernas are lively and pure Greek-island. A good sandy beach stretches right round the bay.

◆◆◆
APOLLÓNIA

Buses regularly travel the 3½ miles (6km) to Apollónia from Kamáres. The old hilltop Chóra, Apollónia is so clean, freshly whitened and neat that it looks modern until you find the narrow lanes and donkey steps of the old town, all painted white.

There are superb views over farmland to the sea from a terrace by a patisserie, where visitors and locals take coffee and wait for buses. Old churches hide in the alleys, and on the hilltop is a blue-domed white church with a domed bell tower. Buses go from Apollónia past farms growing corn, olives and figs, and watch-towers built by Byzantine and Venetian rulers, to the Vrissi monastery at Exambella. Founded in 1614, it possesses precious icons and a little museum of religious art. A left fork beyond here winds down to the fishing hamlet of Pharos (Fáros), 4½ miles (7km) from Apollónia with rooms, two tavernas, and small sandy beaches. A hillside path with

Sífnos pottery makes popular, if bulky, souvenirs of the island

sea views takes you a mile (2km) from here to the monastery of Panagía Chrysopigí on a rocky cape. Near by is a beach taverna famous for fish.

Another bus from Apollónia takes the right fork at Exambella to Platýs Gialós, a tiny resort 6 miles (10km) away. Its long beach is lined with fishermen's cottages, tavernas and bars, two hotels, rooms, and one of two official campsites on Sífnos. The other is on Kamáres bay. The road back to Apollónia passes a convent, Panagía tou Vounóu, with superb sea views. The nuns left last century and you can rent a cell.

◆◆◆
KÁSTRO

The glory of Sífnos is the medieval fortified town of Kástro, set dramatically on a hillside headland over the sea, 3½ miles (5½km) by bus east from Apollónia.

Narrow whitewashed streets and alleys climb the hill, under arches of overhead houses forming bridges leading to upper floors. Pieces of ancient columns and headless busts have been used in making walls. Kástro was capital of Sífnos until 1833. It has survived through classical times, when Herodotus called it a city and it grew rich from its gold and silver mines, and through foreign occupations by Byzantines, Venetians, Franks and Turks, who held it from 1617 to 1834. In classical times Sífnos was one of the biggest contributors to the treasure of the oracle at Delphi, sending each year a golden egg. One year the islanders sent a stone wrapped in gold leaf. The gods showed their wrath by sinking the mines beneath the sea. The island became known for pottery, and potters still work in Kamáres, Vathý and Apollónia.

Over the mountain from Kástro is the 16th-century Chrysostomou monastery, centre of resistance to the Turks.

Sífnos is short of roads or even drivable mule tracks. Nice bays on the west coast can be reached only by hard walking over mountains, or by boat. Caiques go in summer to Vathy, which has a fishing harbour, a sandy beach in a horseshoe bay, a 16th-century church, two tavernas and rooms. Sífnos is a 'connoisseur's' island.

Accommodation

Kamáres: **Stavros**, on the quayside (tel: 0284-31641) is C-class, very friendly, simple and convenient, but the rooms vary a lot. Apollónia: **Sofia**, round the corner from the patisserie, is a good C-class hotel, with restaurant (tel: 0284-31238). **Anthoussa**, over the patisserie, C-class, is modern with lovely views; book early (tel: 0284-31431). **Hotel Sifnos,** Katarati, up the lane opposite the police station (Odos Stylianou Prokou), is C-class (tel: 0284-31624). Platýs Gialós: **Hotel Platýs Gialós**, B-class, clean and comfortable, opens only in summer and you need to book (tel: 0284-71324).

Restaurants

Tavernas on Kamáres waterfront are great fun. Apollónia has a good choice of eating places. The simple taverna next to the patisserie has good cooking and views from its terrace. **Restaurant Cyprus** on the main museum square is smarter and more formal. **Restaurant Krevatina**, in a charming tiny square uphill from the police station, has the most variety of dishes, well cooked, but closes around 14.00hrs until evening. In Kástro, **Zorba's** taverna has fair food.

General Information

Population: 2,100
Area: 32sq miles (82sq km)
76 nautical miles from Piréas
Police: in Apollónia, in an alley off museum square.
Tourist Police: tel: 0284-31210.
Harbour Police: in Kamáres (tel: 0284-31617).

How to Get There

Ferries: Small excursion boats (no cars) go to Páros, where you can pick up boats to other islands: daily, June to September; 2 or 3 times a week in spring and autumn.
Car ferries: 4 days a week from Piréas (via Kýthnos and Sérifos, 6hrs), and on to Kímolos and Mílos; weekly to Folégandros, Síkinos, Íos and Santoríni. Also a connection with Sýros.

SÉRIFOS

Sérifos has never been a tourist island, which makes it particularly attractive to the travellers who do go. At the centre is a mountain, Troúlos, reaching 1,919 feet (585m). Much of the island is bare rock. The main paved road zig-zags 1¾ miles (3km) up to Chóra (Sérifos Town), the old fortified town. Other roads are rough but drivable – but hire cars are scarce. There are several taxis. You can sometimes get lifts on supply trucks. Two buses run only between the port of Livádi and Chóra. The best way to the beaches is by caique.

◆◆
LIVÁDI

Set in a biggish near-horseshoe bay among hills, Livádi is a working fishing port, with the ferry pier and enough tavernas, shops, pensions and rooms to cater for a few tourists and for the yachtsmen who have discovered it. It is a friendly, happy little place, where you can just sit and talk for hours. The slow pace leaves time for thinking, dreaming, reading and resting. There is a beach round the bay, but better ones near by.

CYCLADES

Livakadia beach, reached by a track over a hill behind the ferry quay, is sandy, narrow and treelined, with a surf-riding school in mid-summer. Another half-hour's walk takes you to Karavi beach, which is fairly empty but has some hillside holiday homes. By following the river bed (dry in summer) over a hill you reach Psili Amos, a lovely sandy cove with dunes. In another 15 minutes you reach Ágios Giannis, which is larger but has coarser sand.

◆◆
CHÓRA (SÉRIFOS TOWN)

The old capital, Chóra, a mile (2km) from Livádi, looks spectacular from the port. As well as taking a bus or taxi, you can climb to it up steep wide donkey-steps; the walk down is more fun. To reach the older part of Chóra, you climb steps from the bus-stop square, side-stepping laden mules. You

The best way to see old villages and landscapes on Sérifos is to walk

reach a marble-paved square with a charming church and a large 1908 town hall with iron railings of sculpted swans. Steps spiral up to a crumbling Venetian fort where the whole island population could take refuge from Turkish pirates. A mile past Chóra the road divides. The right hand road, with fine sea views, divides again after the village of Panagía (with a 10th-century Byzantine church) into two rough tracks, dangerous for mopeds. The left leads to a good sandy beach at Sikamia, 4 miles (6km) from Chóra with dunes, clear clean sea and a few buildings. The right track leads to Moní Taxiarchón (Taxiarchón monastery), built in 1600, fortified and painted white with a red dome. It contains Byzantine manuscripts and good 18th-century frescoes. A track leads to a pretty village, Kallistos, with a restaurant. The left-hand fork on the Chóra road also divides. The right

track goes to the old iron and copper mining village of Megálo Livádi, 4½ miles (7km) from Chóra, with ruined buildings, a broad sandy beach and a hamlet with a taverna. The left track leads to Koutalas, a big bay with a shingle shore, a few houses on the back slopes, fishing boats and a taverna. Signs of prehistoric settlement were found in a nearby cave. Legend has it that the rocks of Sérifos used to be the people. The Greek hero Perseus and his mother Danaë landed here after being set adrift in a box. Lecherous King Polydeuces wanted Danaë badly, so he got rid of young Perseus by tricking him into promising to get for him the head of the gorgon Medusa, whose bulging eyes turned men to stone. The goddess Athena gave Perseus a mirror-like shield, winged shoes for quick escape and a cloak which made him invisible. Returning with the head in a sack, he turned the king and his whole court to stone.

Accommodation
Livádi: **Sérifos Beach**, Paralia, C-class (in a cul-de-sac off the quayside), is the best, run by Austrians; booking essential (tel: 0281-51209). **Perseus**, C-class, along the seafront, is beside restaurant Perseus (tel: 0281-51273). **Maistrali**, C-class, is just past Perseus (tel: 0281-51381).

Restaurants
The best tavernas are in the port. Recommended are the restaurant next to the Rock Cocktail Bar, the **Perseus** (over the river bridge) and the

International, on the way to the ferry-boat quay.

General Information
Population: 1,100
Area: 27sq miles (70sq km)
70 nautical miles from Piréas.
Tourist Police: tel: 0281-51300.
Harbour Police: on the Chóra road (tel: 0281-51470).

How to Get There
Ferries: 4 days a week from Piréas (via Kýthnos, 5hrs), and on to Sífnos, Kimolos and Mílos; weekly to Folégandros, Síkinos, Íos and Santoríni. There is also a connection with Sýros. In season, some boats go to Páros, but otherwise you must change at Sífnos.

KÝTHNOS
A few knowledgeable tourists have visited Kýthnos for many years for one reason – the waters of the spa of Loutrá. Those who do go are nearly all Greeks, and there are still very few others. Locals still totally outnumber visitors even in mid-summer in the fishing port of Mérichas, although more yachtsmen are now preferring to explore these three lesser-known and attractive isles of the Cyclades – Sífnos, Sérifos and Kýthnos – rather than the more crowded islands. The result is that Kýthnos' tavernas and hotels are simple and cheap: people seem quite ashamed to take your money. Water can be scarce by the end of the summer.
Buses run in the old Greek Island way – more often by whim than timetable. The best way to get around Kýthnos is by shared taxi. Drivers are helpful.

LOUTRÁ

Loutrá, 5 miles (8km) from Mérichas, has a faded charm despite a new apartment block and a new hotel, and shops are being built. It looks 'ripe for development'. There is already the bungalow-style Xenia-Anagenissis Hotel, with two streams of water running alongside which are brown from iron deposits. One runs at precisely 99°F (37°C) and is used for drinking. The other at 126°F (52°C) is for bathing. They are said to alleviate rheumatism and promote fertility. The spring is under a church next to the baths. Loutrá is still a fishing port, with boats alongside the quay below a church, a tiny castle which is now a private summer home, and rusting iron-mining gear. Over the sands before the quay are simple but lively tavernas.

◆
CHÓRA (KÝTHNOS TOWN)

A modern road from the spa winds up 2 miles (3km) amid fertile land towards Chóra, the old capital, then down 3 miles (5km) more to Mérichas, but you are as likely to see farmers riding donkeys side-saddle as cars. Kýthnos is essentially an old-style agricultural island. Chóra has old white buildings and useful shops, the post office, and a restaurant. But it is dull and has no hotel.

◆◆
MÉRICHAS

A very pleasant and genuine fishing port. Tavernas have tables on the esplanade above a tree-lined but unattractive beach of greyish coarse sand. Ten minutes' walk from the port is a fertile valley leading to a long narrow cove with coarse sand, called Kolóna. It has a taverna and you can walk across a strip of sand to a tiny island. Unfortunately there is some unofficial camping here, with its usual problems of sanitation and litter. You can reach Kolóna by water taxi. The only other road climbs 2½ miles (4km) from Mérichas with fine views to the delightful hillside town of Dryopída, which has narrow, weaving streets and donkey steps with old shops, houses and a few little tavernas. Sudden views appear around corners. You can walk from here to Katafiki cave.

The road continues (and so do occasional buses) 2½ miles (4km) downhill to Kanála, a well-kept little modern resort, with trees to give shade from the noon-day sun and rich in flowers. The fishing boat quay is used also by a few yachts and over a hill is a narrow gritty-sand beach. Here are a pension, rooms, and a café-bar and taverna serving good standard Greek dishes. A relaxing hideout. A monastery here has an icon said to have been painted by St Luke. Several sandy coves round the isle can be reached by boat or on foot, some from Mérichas. San Stephano beach can be reached from Dryopída.

Accommodation

Loutrá: **Kýthnos Bay**, C-class (tel: 0281-31218), is the best

choice here. Mérichas:
Possidonion, C-class, at the
end of the esplanade, is big
(6-storey); many rooms are
booked mid-summer by
Austrian package tours (tel:
0281-32100).

Restaurants
In Loutrá, the beach tavernas
are good, amusing and
good value. In Mérichas there
is nothing outstanding, but
O'Antonis restaurant in a
cul-de-sac opposite the bus-
stop has variety and is friendly.
The **Porto-Bello** on the
esplanade often has lobster or
other good fish, and the **Gialós**
restaurant next door is
considered the smartest eating
place.

General Information
Population: 1,500
Area: 33sq miles (86sq km)
52 nautical miles from Piréas.
Tourist Police: tel: 0281-31201.
Harbour Police: tel: 0281-
31290.

How to Get There
Ferries: From Piréas 4 days a
week (4hrs); Lavrio also on the
mainland (via Kéa) weekly
(4hrs); Sérifos, Sífnos, Kímolos
and Mílos 4 days a week;
weekly to Folégandros, Síkinos,
Íos and Santoríni. There is also
a connection with Sýros.

MÍLOS
Mílos can be disappointing. The
approach into the vast Bay of
Adámas between little islets, past
fishing hamlets and an inviting,
sandy headland to the quay of
Adámas village is very nearly
idyllic. Unfortunately, the
countryside inland is gashed
by the mines and quarries

A sparkling white church in Mílos

which made Mílos rich from
antiquity.

◆
ADÁMAS
The little port, in a ring of hills,
is pretty, with small yachts
flying flags of many nations
coming and going through
Adámas Bay, yet it was big
enough to hold the whole
Allied Fleet of these seas in
World War I. However, the
port can be stifling and dusty
from the mineral ores brought
here for shipment. Most
tourists stay in hotels along
nearby Lanada beach. The
island in the bay, Antímilos, is a
sanctuary for kri-kri (wild
goats) and beyond it are odd
rock formations, such as 'the
bears' (Arkoudes).

◆◆
PLÁKA (MÍLOS TOWN)

The capital, where most islanders live in winter because of flooding, is a short bus-ride up the hill from Adámas. It has two museums. The History and Folk Museum contains interesting relics of island life. The Archaeological Museum has some of the finds from Mílos going back to the neolithic age (*open*: 08.30–15.00hrs; *closed*: Monday). Pláka is believed to be on the site of ancient Milos, destroyed in revenge by the Athenians after the wars with the Spartans whom Milos supported. The men of Milos were killed, women and children enslaved and replaced by Athenian colonists. At the village of Tripiti near Pláka in 1890 British archaeologists unearthed catacombs dating from the island's conversion to Christianity in the 1st century AD. There is a partly excavated Roman theatre.

Venus de Milo

It was in 1820 that a farmer came across a cave near Tripiti. In it was a 2nd-century BC statue of Aphrodite, goddess of love and fertility (Venus to the Romans). The Greeks say that, to save her from the Turks, they lent her to the French for safe keeping. In a scuffle between islanders and the French Navy, she lost her pedestal and arms. The Venus of Mílos (*Venus de Milo*) is now in the Louvre in Paris ('purchased' say the French, 'stolen' say the islanders). The museum in Pláka has only a plaster cast.

◆
ZEFYRÍA

Buses from Pláka go past Adámas along the coast where there are places to swim, then turn inland at an electric power station among mines and machinery to Zefyría, 7 miles (11km) away and capital from the 8th century until 1793. Once it had 5,000 people, 17 churches and two bishops. Pestilence from pirate ships and sulphur fumes from the mines drove out the people.

A rough road used, surprisingly, by buses runs from Zefyría over the hills to Palaiochóri, 10 miles (16km) from Pláka, a beach of grey volcanic sand with several tavernas and a restaurant. The coast road from the power station passes several sandy beaches. The road itself climbs to Moní Agía Marína (Agía Marína monastery) on the side of Mount Profítis Elías. Two beaches north – Phatourena, by a lagoon, and Emborio – can be reached only by boat.

One of the most attractive places on Mílos is the little fishing port of Apollónia in the north, 6 miles (9.5km) from Adámas port and reached by bus. It has Greek holiday homes, rooms to let, tavernas, and a sandy beach. From here you can get a caique to the isle of Kímolos (½hr).

Accommodation

Adámas: **Meltemi**, C-class; near bus square (tel: 0287-22284). **Aphrodite of Mílos**, is a small C-class self-catering establishment (tel: 0297-22020). Pretty **Semiramis** on the waterfront round the bay is D-class, but most rooms have wc-shower (tel: 0287-22117/8).

Restaurants

The best places to eat are in Adámas. **Aphroditis** serves fine sea food and the **Charcoal Taverna** is good value.

General Information

Population: 5,000
Area: 62sq miles (160sq km)
82 nautical miles from Piréas.
Tourist Police: tel: 0287-21378.
Harbour Police: tel: 0287-22100.

How to Get There

Ferries: From Piréas: direct 4 days a week, also 4 days a week via Kýthnos, Sérifos, Sífnos and Kímolos (8hrs); weekly to Íos and Santoríni; Irakleío (Crete) 3 days a week. There is a caique to Páros, July to August.

PÁROS

Páros was near-paradise to knowledgeable travellers 20 years ago: a lively place, with an important little shipping port for inter-island trading, two busy fishing ports, yachts calling but few other tourists. The big sand beaches across the isle were empty, the farms prosperous. Inevitably it has been discovered. There are four or five middle-sized package hotels, an airfield linked with Athens and Crete, and more ferries from Piréas. But it remains delightful, though Paroikiá (Páros Town) port and the fishing village of Náousa are overcrowded in mid-summer. So are buses. Although bus services are good, a hire-car can be very useful. Paroikiá is the busiest ferry-port in the islands, with services in all directions, so Páros is a favourite with island-hoppers.

Píso Livádi is a lively fishing port and resort on Páros

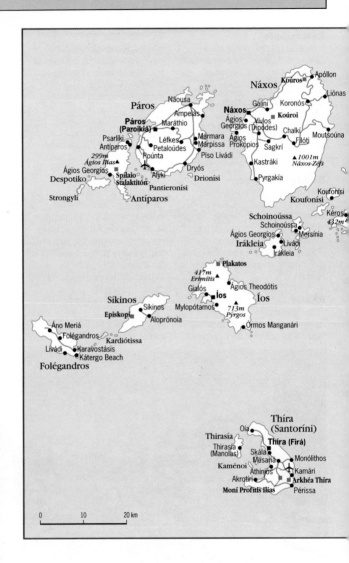

Páros

Náoussa
Ampelás
Maráthio
Páros
(Paroikiá)
Psarlíki
Léfkes
Antíparos
Petaloúdes
Roúnta
299m
Ágios Ilías▲
Ágios Georgíos
Spílaio
Despotiko
Stalaktitón
Alyki
Strongylí
Pantieronísi
Antíparos
Mármara
Márpissa
Ágios
Píso Livádi
Prokópios
Dryós
Drionísi

Náxos
Koúros
Apóllon
Liónas
Gálini
Koronós
Náxos
Koúroi
Ágios
Vívlos
Georgios
(Tripódes)
Chalkí
Filóti
Moutsoúna
Sagkrí
Kastráki
▲1001m
Náxos-Zéfs
Pyrgakía
Koufonísi
Koufonísi
Kéros
432m
Schoinoússa
Schoinoússa
Ágios Georgíos
Mersínia
Irákleia
Livádi
Irákleia

Plakatos
417m
Erímitis▲
Agios Theodótis
Gialós
Íos
Síkinos
Mylopótamos
Íos
Episkopí
713m
Pýrgos
Síkinos
Aloprónoia
Áno Meriá
Órmos Manganári
Folégandros
Kardiótissa
Livádi
Karavostásis
Kátergo Beach
Folégandros

Thíra
(Santoríni)
Oía
Thirasía
Thíra (Firá)
Thirasía
Skála
(Manolas)
Monólithos
Mesariá
Kaménoi
Kamári
Athinjós
Akrotíri
Arkhéa Thíra
Moní Profítis Ilías
Périssa

0   10   20 km

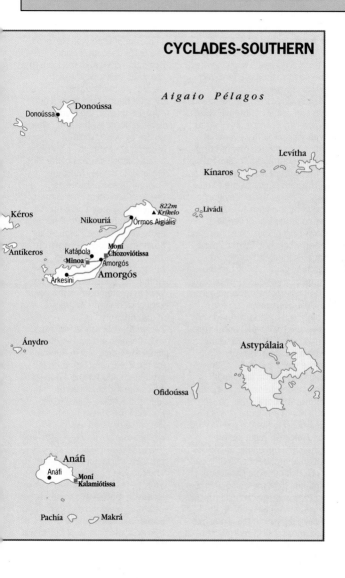

CYCLADES-SOUTHERN

Aigaio Pélagos

Donoússa
Donoússa●

Levítha

Kínaros

Kéros

822m
▲ Kríkelo
Livádi

Nikouriá

Órmos Aigiális

Antíkeros

Katápola
Minoa

Moní
Chozoviótissa
Amorgós
Amorgós

Arkesíni

Ánydro

Astypálaia

Ofidoússa

Anáfi
Anáfi
Moní
Kalamiótissa

Pachía
Makrá

PAROIKIÁ (PÁROS TOWN)

The quayside at Paroikiá where the ferries dock is a working port, and the main square, Plateia Mavrogenous, behind it is a commercial centre, with banks, offices and tavernas crowded with visitors in the evenings. Off it runs the narrow old high street, Lochagou Kortianou, with every sort of little shop.

A maze of white-painted lanes and alleys with donkey-steps leads off the high street, with white houses adorned with flowering plants, churches, and open workshops where men make shoes, furniture and clothes. On a hillock are the ruins of a Venetian fort built in 1260 using Doric columns from a Greek temple. You reach finally an esplanade lined with tavernas and cafés, and a tree-lined beach of sand and shingle with a windsurfing school.

In the town are three 18th-century marble fountains.

The pride of Páros is the **Ekatotapyliani** – the 'church of one hundred doors'. It was designed in the 6th century for the Emperor Justinian by Ignatius, apprentice to Isidore of Miletus, architect of St Sophia's in Constantinople (Istanbul). Ignatius designed it so well that Isidore was jealous and tried to push him off the roof. In the tussle, they both fell. They are commemorated by sculpture at the base of a column in the courtyard. It is said that 99 doors from the church have been found and that when the 100th is found the Greeks will recover Constantinople. Damaged by an earthquake in 1773, the church was restored in the 1960s to its original Byzantine design in the form of a cross. Its bell tower was destroyed in the earthquake, so the bell hangs now from a huge cypress tree. In the National Archaeological Museum (*open*: 08.30–14.00hrs; *closed*: Mondays) next to the church, is a sadly-small section of the Parian Chronicle (Marmor Parium), a social history of Greece carved in Parian marble from 265 BC and discovered in the early 17th century. Much more of it is in the Ashmolean Museum in Oxford (England). There is also a frieze and biography of the satirical poet Archilochos, who invented the iambic pentameter as the best way of delivering his witty blasts at authority.

Parian marble made the island rich. It was used by Pericles to build the Acropolis in Athens, for the Temple of Solomon in Jerusalem and for the *Venus de Milo*. The old quarries at Marathi, 3 miles (5km) from Paroikiá, became uneconomic but were revived in 1844 to supply marble for Napoleon's tomb. You can visit the quarries, but take a light and a sweater. The longest tunnel – 295 feet (90m) – is dark, cold and damp.

Near the medieval capital of Léfkes in the centre of the island, 5½ miles (9km) from Paroikiá, the village of Mármara has streets paved with marble. Márpissa, half a mile (1km) from Mármara, is the prettiest village here. Above its windmills are ruins of a 15th-century Venetian fortress and the 16th-century monastery Ágios Antonios.

◆◆◆
NÁOUSA

Náousa, the fishing port 7½ miles (12km) north of Paroikiá, though no longer peaceful and idyllic, is delightful. In the little working port where fishing boats are packed tight against the sea wall you can eat fish taken literally from boats to the pan. Small hotels and low-rise apartments have been built recently, but in the network of narrow streets off the square houses are typically Cycladic. Several little beaches are within walking distance of Náousa. Ampelás, a fishing village on the east coast, 3 miles (5km) from Náousa, has a beach and is becoming a small resort with hotels.

Píso Livádi, 13 miles (21km) from Paroikiá across the island, is a pleasant, lively fishing port and resort in summer, almost deserted in winter. The quay and beach are backed by tavernas and little hotels. South from here along the coast are five beaches which you can walk along. There is a bus, usually crowded. Logaros beach has lovely sands and tavernas. Chrysí Aktí has long golden sands and is the best beach on the island. Dryós, where the bus turns back, is an old fruit-growing village turned into a posh little resort where Athenians have summer villas. Several beaches beyond are often deserted.

◆
ALYKÍ

Through beautiful farmland above seascapes you reach Alykí, joined to Paroikiá 7½ miles

The ever-popular 'Greek' salad for lunch at a taverna in the inner harbour, Náousa

(12km) away by a paved road. A fishing village with a lovely tree-lined sandy beach, it is growing fast, with hotels, tavernas, several restaurants, a disco and cement-block villas built by Athenians. The airport is here, with direct flights to Athens, and it is expanding to take bigger planes.

◆
POÚNTA

The road runs on to Poúnta, a little village with a good hotel, bars, tavernas and a big quay, 6¼ miles (10km) from Paroikiá. Little ferries shuttle between here and the small isle of Antíparos (see page 43) a 10-minute journey. Yachtsmen should beware – currents are strong and winds tricky.

The lush valley Petaloúdes behind Poúnta, with its thick woods and constantly-running stream, is known as the Valley of Butterflies. Like those on Rhodes, the scarlet-winged creatures are in fact moths. Try to avoid July and August in Páros. In other months it is charming.

Accommodation

The A-class **Léfkes Village** (tel: 0284-41827), is small and elegant. Paroikiá: **Georgy**, Plateia Mavrogenous, central; C-class, rooms with wc, shower (tel: 0284-21667). **Dina**, just off Plateia Velentza by Ágios Triada Church, E-class but charming with garden (tel: 0284-21325). Náousa: **Hotel Aliprantis**, C-class, excellent position on main square, rooms with wc, shower (tel: 0284-51571). **Minoa**, Ágios Panteleimonou (south end of town), C-class, rooms with balconies, good restaurant (tel: 0284-51309). Ágios Argiti, ½ mile (1km) from Náousa: **Calypso**, overlooking sandy beach, C-class (tel: 0284-51488). Píso Livádi: **Márpissa**, B-class pension, (tel: 0284-41288). **Leto**, C-class (tel: 0284-41283).

Campsites: Koula (at Paroikiá), open April to October; restaurant, supermarket, showers (tel: 0284-22081/2). Capt. Cafkis Camping (at Píso Livádi), pool, supermarket, café (tel: 0284-41392/5).

Restaurants

Paroikiá: **To Tamarisko**, Odos Agorakritou, is still probably the best on the island. **Kriako's** in the high street, is good and

pricey. **Limanaki** is probably best of those along the tourist beach southwest of the ferry quay, with good fish. **Restaurant Argonauta** beside the Bank of Commerce in Mavrogenous Square, serves good dishes. Above is a good-value clean hotel (rooms with wc and shower) but often full. Náousa: there are very good seafood tavernas by the harbour. **Christos Taverna** at the top of the High Street is excellent.

General Information

Population: 8,000
Area: 81sq miles (209sq km)
95 nautical miles from Piréas.
Tourist Office: tel: 0284-22679.
Tourist Police: 24 Plateia Mavrogenous (tel: 0284-21673).
Harbour Police: tel: 0284-21240.

How to Get There

Air: Two flights daily from Athens, more in July to August (50mins). To Irakleío (Crete) 1 May to September, 3 days a week (45mins); Rhodes 4 days a week (1hr 10 mins).
Ferries: From Piréas 1–3 sailings daily May to September, 5 days a week in winter (7hrs). 'No-car' ferry to Sífnos daily, useful also for changing ferries to Sérifos, Kýthnos and other isles. Daily ferries to Íos, Santoríni and Náxos. Other ferries to Amorgós, (5 days a week), Astypálaia, Ikaría, Irákleia, Schoinoússa, Koufonísi, Mýkonos (all 3 days a week), Folégandros, Síkinos, Kálymnos, Kós, Nísyros, Tílos, Sými, Rhodes, Crete, Kárpathos, Kásos, Sýros and Donoússsa (once a week). Also many excursion boats in summer.

The clear water of the fishing harbour, Antíparos

ANTÍPAROS

Until recently, people went to Antíparos almost entirely to look at the cave at Spílaio. Now backpackers in particular go for the near-deserted beaches and clear waters. No cars are allowed, although mopeds are on hire in mid-summer – a noisy hazard. The tree-lined harbour, with a windmill (now a disco) and white fishermen's chapel, has beautifully clear water. It is a five-minute walk from the only real settlement, the attractive old Venetian fortified town of Kástro, and nearly all the tavernas, shops, hotels, etc are on the quay, in the town, or along the connecting road.

◆◆
SPÍLAIO STALAKTITÓN (SPÍLAIO CAVES)

The only road goes to Spílaio, a two-hour thirsty tramp. But you can get a caique from the ferry quay most of the year.

The cave entrance is a half-hour's slog up the slopes of Mount Ágios Ilías, which rises to 751 feet (229m). But teams of mules await to give you a ride – pricey but well worth it. The entrance is by a church. Once visitors went down and up by rope. Now there are 400 cement steps. The cave is dark, dripping, cold and eerie. Stalactites and stalagmites up to 10 feet (3m) long have survived centuries of looting by souvenir hunters, graffiti writers and even German hand grenades in 1941–5. Refugees have hidden in this cave since men fled here from the wrath of the Macedonian Alexander the Great.

A graffiti inscription in Latin records a Christmas Mass celebrated here in 1673 for the French Ambassador to Constantinople, Count Nouantelle, who paid 500 Parians and Antiparians to attend. A true eccentric, he then had Christmas dinner aboard the pirate-ship of Daniel of Malta.

Accommodation

Chryssi Akti on the Kástro beach, C-class, is elegant and the best hotel (tel: 0284-61206). **Mantalena**, Kástro, D-class, has some rooms with wc, showers (tel: 0284-61220).

Restaurants

Antíparos is not very good for eating. **Yorgos** taverna in Kástro is the most popular.

General Information

Population: 650
Area: 13½sq miles (35sq km)
Tourist Office & Tourist Police: Kástro (tel: 0284-61202).

How to Get There

Ferries: Taxi-ferry from Poúnta on Páros (10mins). Summer caiques 1–3 daily from Paroikiá, Páros (40mins).

NÁXOS ✓

Biggest of the Cyclades, Náxos has been blessed by nature. Its mountains are greener and more beautiful than the rugged mountains of Crete. Even when the mountain rivers and waterfalls run dry in summer, they are a riot of oleander flowers. The green fertile plains produce lemons, olives, nuts, · grapes, flowers and vegetables. Its beaches are superb.
Bus services are not bad, but a good way of getting around Náxos in summer is to hire a mini-moke. Closed cars can be too hot, and scooters are dangerous on the dirt roads.

◆
CHÓRA (NÁXOS TOWN)

The port and capital, Náxos is a working town, with tourism and beauty second to commerce. The narrow streets of the medieval town uphill from the harbour are dark and can look sinister. Within the walls of the old Chóra are Venetian houses, doorways and coats-of-arms, and on the hilltop sit a Venetian *kástro*, a Ducal palace and other Italian palazzi. An Italian freebooter, Marco Sanuda, took the isle in 1207, became Duke of Náxos and ruler of several Cycladian isles.
The harbour has plenty of tavernas, bars, restaurants and shops around it. From here they export wine, olive oil, grain and figs. The lemon trade has died off, but they make a sweet and sour liqueur called Kitrou from lemon leaves – four varieties and colours from slightly to very sweet. The people of Náxos make above average wines, too (Promponas red, rosé and white are palatable, Ariadne better). And so they should, for Dionysus (Bacchus, god of wine) taught them. He sailed in one fine day to find Ariadne, daughter of King Minos of Crete, lying asleep on a beach. She had fled with Theseus after helping him slay the Minotaur in the maze, but he abandoned her on Náxos while she slept, sailing sneakily for Athens. But Dionysus found the sunbathing beauty and seduced her. A festival dedicated to Dionysus is held in mid-August in Náxos's main square.
The one Classical Greek touch in the port is an 18-foot- (5.5m) high marble doorway on an islet joined by a causeway – all that remains of a temple of Apollo begun in 522 BC and never finished.

Ágios Geórgios beach, long, with dunes, is almost a suburb of Náxos, with hotels, bars and discos. Agía Anna, accessible by bus or caique, is popular too. A 15-minute walk north from here is the quieter Ágios Prokópios. All these beaches have rooms, as has Kastráki, south by an unpaved road, with a hamlet and beach taverna. South from here, with a paved road back to Náxos, is Pirgakía, with a fine sand beach.

The Pirgakía–Náxos road goes through Sagkrí, 6 miles (10km) from Náxos, hamlets of old houses in cobbled streets encircled by castles, windmills and ruined by Byzantine and Venetian villas. A left road leads to Tripódes (Vívlos), a large, attractive village where wine is produced. Near by is Ágios Mamos, a recently restored 8th-century cathedral with remarkable 7th-century icons. The other road from Sagkrí goes through attractive country to Chalkí, 10 miles (16km) from Náxos, a pretty village, centre for old Venetian castles and Byzantine churches. The route becomes spectacular, with gorgeous mountain views, to Filóti, largest village on the island, on the slopes of Mount Náxos-Zéfs. The road zig-zags to high villages, and you can take a truly rough snaking road to Moutsoúna, an old east-coast port with a shingle beach, taverna and old sheds. The main road winds north through the mountains to the highest village Koronís, pretty with lovely views of woods, fields and mountain streams, then drops down to the delightful fishing port of Apóllon 18½ miles (30km) from Náxos.

The attractive waterfront at Náxos is lined with bars, tavernas, restaurants, shops and hotels

APÓLLON

This village is still typically 'Greek-island', with fishing caiques slapping against the quayside, tavernas on the quay road, houses and hotels on the shingle beach beyond rocks; no-one hurrying, everyone finding time for a chat or an ouzo. But in high summer excursion coaches now arrive from Náxos, so it is at its best before midday or in the evening, when the far from serious business of eating and drinking begins in the tavernas. While the excursionists are there, you can walk to sandy coves or to the old marble quarries to see the *kouros*, a sculpted figure of a man 34½ feet (10.5m) high, made around 650 BC but uncompleted. You can see better but smaller *kouroi* ('young men') at Flerio, 3 miles (5km) northeast of Náxos. They are 16½ feet (5m) tall, are marching with their arms down and may have been guardians of Zeus, father of the gods.

From Apóllon runs a rough coastal road round the north and west coasts, with spectacular scenery. A series of attractive coves begins with Ormos Abram, a farming village by a pebble beach, with a pension. Other beaches include Chilia Voyssi, with tracks to two coves, and Galíni, where a valley path leads to an attractive cove. From here the road to Náxos is paved.

Accommodation

There are plenty of hotels, pensions and rooms in Náxos and at nearby beaches. In Náxos, the **Ariadne**, 1 Ariadnis Street, is a C-class hotel with fine harbour views (tel: 0285-22452). **Panorama**, Amphitritis Kástro, C-class, has super sea views and some rooms with WC, shower (tel: 0285-24404).

Restaurants

There is plenty of choice, especially in Náxos and at Ágios Georgíos beach, of places to eat. **Taverna Karvagio** on Paralia Ariadnis has a wide choice of good dishes. **Meltemi Restaurant** close to it is a favourite.

General Information

Population: 14,000
Area: 173sq miles (448sq km)
106 nautical miles from Piréas.
Tourist Office & Tourist Police: in Náxos (tel: (0285-22100).
Harbour Police: tel: 0285-22300.

How to Get There

Ferries: From Piréas (via Páros) 2 sailings most days (8hrs); from Íos and Santoríni 1–2 sailings a day; from Mýkonos (non-car vessel) 4 days a week; from Rafina daily (6½hrs). Other ferries go on various days to Irakleío (Crete), Schoinoússa, Koufonísi, Donoússa, Amorgós, Sýros and Astypálaia. A little motor vessel (no cars) goes twice a week to Crete, Donoússa and Amorgós.

ÍOS

The little isle of Íos, once peaceful and idyllic, has gone through the sound barrier in a few years. It is still a delight to the young who worship sun, sand, sex, souvlaki and sound. If you value peace, do not go to Íos between Easter and September.

There is a little port, Gialós, a startlingly white, old town (Chóra) with dozens of little domed churches amid alleyways and steep lanes, reached from the port by a paved road or steep mule track, and superb beaches. There are also a mass of tourist shops and disco bars belting out loud rhythms until dawn. The crowds have brought an acute water shortage, affecting sewerage.

◆
MYLOPÓTAMOS

The excellent Mylopótamos beach, deserted not long ago, has restaurants, cafés, bars, two campsites, several small hotels and a supermarket. Here most of the young sleep until early evening, so that it is difficult not to tread on them if you want to reach the water.

Buses from the port to the Chóra now continue to this beach. Invasions started with the arrival of the flower children in the late 1960s. They were friendly, peaceful and broke, so that they slept on the beach, but caused no trouble. There was one disco in a deserted windmill and classical music at the Íos Club. Íos was overrun with young people, many of them hippies. Beaches were fouled, litter accumulated, mosquitoes and flies multiplied, drugs brought thievery and fights. Naturally, the police got tough. They stopped beach-sleeping, and put hippies on return boats. Now most visitors are young people who have money for beds and food. They have a wonderful time dancing until dawn and sleeping by day. The great awakening comes in early evening as they wander into bars for their first drink or to their rooms for a shower before the evening action. It is the nightly noise which drives away the older devotees of Íos.

Less crowded than Mylopótamos bay is the sandy Ágios Theodótis beach 6 miles (10km) across the island, but it is getting more popular. A rough road leads to it, but it takes around three hours to walk. A bus runs once a day in summer. It has a taverna, rooms of what are called 'Indian Huts', which are the stone huts of a long-forgotten attempt to set up a sort of Club Mediterranée here. You can reach Manganári beach in the south only by boat from the port (50 minutes each way).

Mylopótamos beach throngs with bronzing bodies by day and sleeping souls by night

Here there are two tavernas and a fairly pricey German-built hotel with restaurant and disco.

There is little to see on Íos, and no transport except buses and walking. Above Ágios Theodótis beach are the ruins of a Venetian medieval fortress and a monastery where the people hid from pirates. Homer is said to have died on Íos, and enthusiasts go by donkey or on foot (2–3hrs) to Plakatos in the north, on the slopes of Mount Erimítis, where his tomb was said to be.

◆◆
SÍKINOS

Two ferries a week *en route* from Piréas to Íos call at the nearby island of Síkinos, and there are some boat excursions from Íos in summer. It is a very simple isle, living from land and sea, with mules and donkeys doing the fetching and carrying. There are no cars or buses yet. It has a delightful Chóra and deserted beaches in the south.

Accommodation

Nissos Íos, on Mylopótamos beach, C-class (tel: 0286-91306). **Delfini**, Mylopótamos beach, is more civilised than most, C-class (tel: 0286-91340/1). **Aktaeon**, over Acteon Travel office on port square, D-class (tel: 0286-91207). **Armadoros**, smart C-class (tel: 0286-91201). **Manganári Bungalows**, B-class, (tel: 0286-91200), offers the best self-catering accommodation at Manganari. Chóra: **Afroditi** on beach road, good D-class (tel: 0286-91546).

Restaurants

Simple, but best for food, is probably **Draco's Taverna** (*not* Dracos Restaurant) by Mylopótamos beach, noted for fish. It is also a pension (tel: 028-91243).

General Information

Population: 1,450
Area: 41½sq miles (108sq km)
107 nautical miles from Piréas.
Tourist Office & Tourist Police: Town Hall, Chóra (tel: 0286-91222).
Harbour Police: tel: 0286-91264.

How to Get There

Ferries: Almost daily from Piréas in summer, 2–3 times a week in winter (11hrs); daily to Santoríni, Náxos (3hrs) and Páros (5hrs); twice a week to Síkinos, Folégandros and Sífnos; twice a week to Sérifos and Sýros (1hr); once a week to Tínos and Mílos. Small boats go to Síkinos (45mins).

THÍRA (SANTORÍNI)

Santoríni, as the island is best known to visitors, is spectacular, dramatic – sinister to some – but interesting. Crescent shaped, it is the surviving land of a volcanic eruption of around 1600 BC which sunk the rest of the isle in the bay, leaving three smaller isles, two of which (Kameni isles) are still actively volcanic. The tidal wave from the eruption is believed to have destroyed the Minoan cities of Crete. Smaller eruptions have followed through the centuries, the last in 1956. Much of the isle is covered with pumice and lava, and beaches are of 'black' (grey) volcanic dust.

◆◆
THÍRA (FIRÁ)

The town of Thíra (Thera or Firá), spread along a cliff above the old ferry port, Skála, is very attractive, despite being almost totally rebuilt after the 1956 earthquake. Exploring the town in daytime is purgatory. Most shops sell souvenirs or tourist clothes and fanatical sales touts not only pester you but almost drag you into their shops. Restaurants hurry you through meals, too, as if they need your table. The reason is that cruise ships and excursions from other isles pour their passengers into the town all day. After the shops shut, you can admire Thíra – a white cubist town on terraces,

Startlingly white modern churches rise up on terraces above Thíra

with pretty churches between houses. Views are superb, and restaurants are sited so that you can eat and admire them. For superb views and good food, eat at Leschis. When excursion boats cease in October, Thíra shuts down until early May. Winters are terrible on Santoríni. Gales and fierce seas can cut it off, even by air.

The Archaeological Museum has vases and jars excavated at Arkhéa (Ancient) Thíra and Akrotíri, and Roman sculptures (*open*: 08.30–15.00hrs; *closed*: Mondays). In the Orthodox cathedral is a museum of ecclesiastical relics.

Happily there is now a cable car up the cliff (886ft/270m high with 587 steps) from Skála to Thíra. You can still go up the old way, by mule, but the muleteers

CYCLADES

must be some of the nastiest people in the Greek Islands, beating their animals, rarely resting or watering them during the day, and deliberately running into people who prefer to walk up. Most ferries now put into another port, Athiniós, which is linked to Thíra by bus.

◆◆◆
AKROTÍRI

On the road from Thíra to the interesting archaeological site at Akrotíri are hotels and pensions, notably at Karterados, 1¼ miles (2km) from Thíra, served by a good bus service, and at Mesariá, 3¾ miles (6km) from Thíra. Roads lead to a volcanic-dust beach at Monólithos, where there are two tavernas and a canning factory, and to the port-resort of Kamári. Excavations at Akrotíri, 8½ miles (14km) from Thíra, were started in 1967 by a Greek, Professor Marinatos. He died in 1974 and is buried here. For a good study of the site, read the book by his son Dr Manos Marinatos, *Art and Religion in Thera – Reconstructing a Bronze Age Society*. Thera is the name most used by the Greeks for Santoríni. A Minoan town from around 1600 BC has been unearthed. It is not quite so impressive as Knossos on Crete, but has buildings up to three storeys high, even doors, window frames and water systems, preserved under the lava. It is of the same period as Knossos and proves the close connection with Crete, 128 miles (205km) away. The frescoes discovered at Akrotíri, including a springtime scene of birds and flowers covering

Santoríni's black beaches (this is Kamári), caused by volcanic activity, do not put sun-worshippers off

three walls, are, alas, in Athens. The site's roofing can make it very hot at mid-day. It shuts around 15.00hrs and closes on Mondays. Below is a bay of pebbles and rock with a good hotel (the Akrotíri, tel: 0286-81375), and a taverna and village above with bars and rooms among vineyards.

remains of ancient Thera, which you reach by tackling a mountain path from either side. The ruins were excavated from 1867 and date mostly from 300–145 BC, when the Egyptians had a naval base at Kamári, though there was a city here 600 years earlier; erotic carvings on rocks date from the 7th century BC. Remains include temples to the Egyptian gods Isis, Seraphis and Anubis, to Dionysus, god of wine, Apollo and the Egyptian Ptolemies; a theatre with a frightening sheer drop to the sea; and inscriptions from around 800 BC, recording names of participants at the *gymnopaidia* when young soldiers took part in athletic contests and nude dancing.

◆
KAMÁRI

Kamári, until recently a charming fishing village with a big 'black' beach and a few hotels and tavernas, has grown into a lively resort devoted mostly to young holiday-makers, with music bars with names like Banana Moon, dancing until dawn in nightspots, waterskiing, pedaloes and surfing from the beach. A stiff mountain path from here leads to the 17th-century monastery of Profítis Ilías at 1,857 feet (566m). It has a museum of icons, paintings and relics.

◆
PÉRISSA

A road across the isle leads to Périssa (9¼ miles/15km from Thíra; bus), with a black sandy beach, small hotels, rooms and tavernas. The big modern church is on the site of the Byzantine church to St Irene, from whom the name Santoríni came. The mountainous headland dividing Périssa from the beach resort of Kamári (6 miles/10km from Thíra; bus), has the

◆
ATHINIÓS

Now the main ferry port, lying 7½ miles (12km) south of Thíra on the west coast, this has a ferry pier, bars and little else. Swarms of hotel buses meet the ferries.

Artefacts from the substantial Minoan town which has been excavated at Akrotíri, Santoríni

OÍA

The third port, Oía (Ia), 6¾ miles (11km) north of Thíra, was ruined by the last earthquake but, thanks to tourism, has been very attractively restored, with smart restaurants, shops, bars and accommodation in traditional cave-houses.

Accommodation

Thíra: **Atlantis**, A-class, spectacular views, pricey (tel: 0286-22232). **Panorama**, 1¼ miles (2km) north of town, C-class, superb views (tel: 0286-22481). **Tataki**, in a lane from Plateia Theokopoulou (bus square) past Pelikan Tours, has rooms with showers and is good for D-class (tel: 0286-22389). Karterados (1¼ miles (2km) from Thíra): **Loizos**, C-class, all rooms have WC, shower (tel: 0286-31733). Kamári: all grades of hotels. Oía: **Archontiko Argyron** (tel: 0286-31669), in restored mansion. A-class. The remarkable cave houses of the **Tsitouras Collection** are luxurious, unique and packed with antiques and works of art. A-class.

Restaurants

The isle is proud of its wine. Nichteri is white and dry, Vinsanto white, sweet and strong. There is plenty of choice of eating places in Thíra. Prices are rather high but meals are good. **Castro**, near the cable car, is good and pricey. **Nicholas Taverna** (just down the port steps) is cheap and may have a queue. In Oía, **George's** is good value. Kamári has many tavernas.

General Information

Population: 7,000
Area: 37sq miles (96sq km)
127 nautical miles from Piréas.
No tourist police.
Town Police: tel: 0286-22649.
Harbour Police: Odos 25 March, Thira (tel: 0286-22239).

How to Get There

Air: International charters and package tours fly direct. There are flights from Athens 2 or 3 times a day in summer (55mins), from Mykonos daily (40mins), from Crete 4 times a week (40mins) and from Rhodes three times a week (1hr).
Ferries: From Piréas (12hrs) daily, often twice a day in summer. Daily (often two boats) to Íos, Páros and Náxos; Crete 5 days a week; Mýkonos 4 days a week; 2 days a week to Síkinos, Sýros and Folégandros. Twice a week to Sífnos and Sérifos. Once a week to Tínos, Kímolos, Mílos and Kýthnos.

IONIAN ISLES

ZÁKYNTHOS (ZANTE) ✓

Despite the earthquake of 1953 which destroyed most of its Venetian buildings, and a new airfield which brings a major annual invasion of package tourists, Zákynthos is still attractive.

Most package tour visitors stay either in Laganás, Argási, or Alikés in the north, which have become tourism boom towns. All these have some seasonal nightlife. The capital port, Zákynthos Town, is happy and quite lively. The rest of the island is relaxed and sleepy with little isolated, deserted beaches and hamlets where goats, sheep, olive trees and vines take precedence over visitors. Roads are reasonably paved for exploring much of the island, but if you take to the other 'roads' which are really dirt mule tracks, especially in the hilly north of the isle, you will find life slips back two centuries. A hire car is very rewarding but a little courage is needed to tackle some roads. Wells and springs have made valleys fertile and green.

Provided that there is reasonable soil and a regular supply of water, more or less anything will grow in the sheltered valleys of Zákynthos

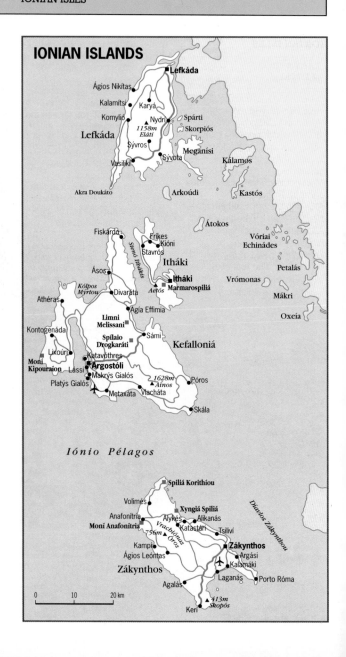

◆◆
ZÁKYNTHOS TOWN

Rebuilt after the earthquake in
its Venetian pattern, with
arcades, squares, narrow
streets and little palazzi, the
town is in a lovely position
among hills. The elegant rebuilt
main square, Plateia Solomou,
is named after the poet
Dionysos Solomos, who died in
1857. He wrote the Greek
national anthem, 'Hymn of
Liberty', translated into English
by Rudyard Kipling. Like Corfu,
Zákynthos was governed by the
English from 1809 to 1864.
The lovely 15th-century Ágios
Nikólaos Church in the corner
of the square is one of the few
that could be restored after the
earthquake.
Fine icons (15th–19th century)
saved from wrecked churches
are in the Art Museum on the
square, with religious paintings
of the Ionian School by artists
who fled from the Turks in
Crete (*open*: 08.30–15.00hrs;
closed: Mondays). Kástro, the
hillside Venetian castle, also
survived the earthquake. You
have a good view of town, bay
and mainland coast from up
there, but it can be windy
(*open*: 08.30–14.30hrs; *closed*:
Mondays).
Zákynthos is a busy little
commercial port, with cargo
ships and ferries docking
beside a harbour pier or right
on the portside, which is lined
with cafés, tavernas and
souvenir shops specialising in
woollen sweaters, local nougat,
perfumes and liqueurs. Fishing
boats land their catch, too. At
the opposite end from the ferry
quay is the most impressive

*Zákynthos Town has a clear
indigenous life of its own, quite
separate from the demands of
tourism*

church, the rebuilt St Dionysios,
named after the island's patron.
With its red roof and square
white bell tower, it looks as
pretty in daytime against the
blue summer sky as it does lit at
night and shining in the water.
The inside, lit by chandeliers, is
blue and white with ornate,
many-coloured frescoes on its
curved ceiling.
The narrow roads behind the
harbour are full of typically
Greek-island shops in
apparent disorder, cafés,
restaurants, a few hotels and
the bus station with fairly good
services to several parts of the
island. Restaurants and night
life are centred on Ágios
Marko square.

◆◆
LAGANÁS

Laganás lures Greeks from the Peloponnese mainland as well as thousands of foreigners, so its 5½ miles (9km) of soft, gently-shelving sand are overcrowded in summer. It has a good choice of tavernas beside the beach, and bars, tavernas and restaurants on the main road. Watersports are available, there is a disco, an open air cinema and a regular bus service into the town. It is a good place for families or lively young people, and is to be found 4½ miles (7km) south of the port.

◆◆
ARGÁSI

A developing village, but more relaxed than Laganás and set in more attractive scenery. Its sand and pebble beach is narrow but the bay is attractive, with

Summer sunset across Defni Bay, Zákynthos

translucent, clean water and a sandy seabed. There are several shops, some good tavernas and restaurants, bars with music nightly and discos which come and go each season. One is in an old Venetian mansion. The main road can be quite busy in summer but it is a relaxed place, with watersports. Behind is Mount Skopós which men would climb in days past to watch for pirate ships. Argási is 2½ miles (4km) from Zákynthos.

◆
KALAMÁKI

Over the mountain, 3 miles (5km) from Zákynthos, is Kalamáki, a typically Greek village with a long, wide sandy beach just starting to be developed. There are new studios, a couple of hotels, bars, a restaurant and a disco.
The hilly road from Argási leads to attractive beaches with simple tavernas – St Nicholas and delightful Porto Róma, with a fine

sweep of sand in a wooded bay. The road becomes a drivable track leading to the clean, golden sands of Vasilikós beach.

Loggerhead Turtles

Parts of Laganás Bay and Vasilikós are rightly closed to people, for there are more important visitors. For millions of years loggerhead turtles, endangered giants of the sea, have come in at night in early summer to lay their eggs. So please keep away and leave the beaches to the turtles.

◆

TSILIVÍ

Northward from Zákynthos Town is a lush, fertile plain of orange and olive groves, and vines producing grapes for the famous Zante currants, known to Elizabethans in England. In the spring, wild flowers are lovely here. Three miles (5km) from Zákynthos Town is the farming village of Tsiliví, where olive trees meet a beach of sand as fine as talcum powder. There are two small hotels, tavernas, holiday villas and a pub.

◆◆

ALIKÉS

Alikés bay has a superb stretch of sand backed by dunes and salt lagoons, with lovely country behind rising to the mountains. The little resort of Alikés at the eastern end is still uncommercialised, though it has the usual tavernas, tourist shops, bars and even a small roller-skating rink. There are watersports available too. Alikanás, a mile away, is an even smaller place.

SIGHTS

At the northern tip of the island are **Spiliá Korithíou** (Kianou Caves), known as the Blue Grotto. Go in the afternoon when the sun shining on the azure sea makes patterns in shades of blue on the cave walls. In summer, caique trips go to the caves from Alikés, or you can reach them by taking a road to the sea at Volimés, with two tavernas, sands which get very hot, and a quay where small boats sail to the caves. Further south is Xyngía Spiliá, a big sandy bay called Smugglers' Cove, visited usually by boat from Alikés, half way round the island, for there is no road to it. The wreck of a large ship rusts in the sands – rumoured to be the debris of a fortuitous insurance *coup*. The main road from Zákynthos Town, bypassing Laganás, reaches the natural pitch-wells of **Kerí**, used from ancient times until recently for caulking boats and mentioned by both Pliny and Herodotus. At Keri village are fine views, and the beach below has two tavernas. **Moní Anafonítrias**, the 15th-century Monastery of Anafonítrias, is 5 miles (8km) from Katastári, inland from Alikés. It withstood the earthquake and is kept by nuns who will show you the frescoes, medieval tower and cell of Dionysios, patron saint of Zákynthos.

On the west side, downhill from Ágios Leóntas, is the quiet village of Kampí. A track winds uphill to a sadly dramatic scene. Below a sheer clifftop is a tiny bay with near-violet seas lapping grey rocks. On a peak behind is a massive concrete cross. It is a memorial to Greek freedom fighters who were thrown over the cliff in World War II. Incongruously there is a small modern bar-taverna here.

Festivals
Carnival is held two weeks before Lent, with masked singers and dancing. 24 August is the festival of St Dionysios.

Accommodation
The best hotel in Zákynthos Town is **Diana Palace**, A-class, (tel: 0695-23070). **Xenia**, 66 Dionissiou Roma (tel: 0695-22232/22666), B-class, is hidden in a narrow street. A reliable C-class hotel is the **Aegli**, 12 Lomvardou Street (tel: 0695-28317). **Strada Marina**, 14 K Lomvardou Street, on the quay with sea and harbour views (tel: 0695-22761/3), B-class, is good value. Alikés: The **Asteria** (tel: 0695-83203), C-class, is comfortable and right beside the beach. Argási: The A-class **Akti Zakantha** (tel: 0695-26441/3) is modern with seaview balconies. **Chryssi Akti** (tel: 0695-28679) overlooks the beach, with terrace and balconies. **Argási Beach Hotel** (tel: 0695-28554), also right on the beach has a pleasant bar (C-class). The **Mimoza Beach** (tel: 0695-22588) has bedrooms in chalets and a good restaurant overlooking the sea. Laganás: a big choice of hotels and pensions. Kalamáki: **Crystal Beach** (tel: 0695-22917), C-class, is family-run, friendly, in good surroundings beside a beach. Tsiliví: **Hotel Tsiliví** (tel: 0695-23109) is box-like and small, but friendly.

The path to the beach from the White Rocks Hotel, Kefalloniá

Restaurants
Zákynthos produces a good local white wine, Verdea, as well as a local brandy, ouzo and strawberry liqueur. Meals on the island are well above average, especially in beach resorts and Zákynthos Town, though among the restaurants around Ágios Marko square and the town hall are some less up-market places – pizza and Greek fast food establishments.
Eat well at **Petas Evangelos**, Alex Roma Street, where food is freshly prepared and the service enthusiastic.

KEFALLONIÁ ✓

Kefalloniá has been described as an island of dramatic mountainous beauty and ugly prefabricated buildings. Nature is responsible for both. It suffered even more than Zákynthos from the 1953 earthquake, so few remains are left of its Mycenaean and Classical past, or of its Venetian heritage of fine buildings. It lives by trade, shipping and agriculture, not tourism, so that its capital and main port, Argostóli, has been rebuilt as a working city, not for the convenience or delight of tourists. The town's beaches and coves and most tourist hotels are a 1¾-mile (3km) bus ride away. But the centre and north of the island have awesome mountain drives with good views.

◆◆
ARGOSTÓLI

Argostóli is busy with a big market, shops, bars, cafés and restaurants, providing for locals rather than visitors, around the attractive modern Ioannou Metaxa Square. Metaxa was a local man: dictator of Greece in 1940, he defied the Italian dictator Mussolini and became a Greek hero.
Argostóli was famous pre-1953 for its bell towers, and a few have been rebuilt, notably the German-style tower of the Catholic church near the square. When the British administered these isles, they built the Drapanos bridge across the narrow gulf, with low arches, leaving a good fishing lagoon. It

General Information
Population: 32,000
Area: 161sq miles (417sq km)
Tourist Office & Tourist Police: at town hall (tel: 0695-22200).
Harbour Police: tel: 0695-22417.

How to Get There
Air: From Athens (2–6 flights daily); from Kefalloniá (2–3 weekly). Charter flights from many European countries from mid-April to mid-October.
Ferries: 3 daily (6–9 in summer) to Kyllini on the Peloponnese coast (1¼hrs). Some boats go in summer to Argostóli on Kefalloniá; speed boats go to Patras in summer.
Coach: Athens via Kyllini (7hrs).

leads to the little Lássi peninsula and the geological oddity called Katavóthres (swallow holes), where the sea is sucked into two large tunnels under the ground. They were long used for driving sea mills. Since the earthquake they have become a trickle. No-one knew where the water went until 1963, when a geologist poured in a lot of dye. Fifteen days later it appeared in the lake of Melissani cave and near Sámi, right across the island. Across Lássi peninsula above the lagoon are the high walls of the 7th-century BC acropolis of Krani. The best organised beaches are at Lássi, and also 2–3 miles (3–5 km) south of Argostóli (Makrýs Gialós and Platýs Gialós), on the airport road. Buses run regularly from mid-June to mid-September. Bus services are reasonable on Kefalloniá; in summer, taxis are numerous and boats go to popular beaches.

◆◆
LIXOÚRI

A car ferry goes 12 times a day (8 on Sundays) from Argostóli to the quiet little port of Lixoúri across the gulf (½hr, or 20 miles round by road). Rebuilt, with wide streets, it is a pleasant town divided by a river and centred round a little square. It has its own fishing boats, so its tavernas serve good fish. (Try Anthony's, by the ferry: good food and he speaks English well.) Beaches are along the coast southwards, mostly in little sandy coves. Across the peninsula is Moní Kipouríon (Kipoureon monastery) in its lovely setting, with guest cells.

◆◆
PÓROS

Ferries from Kyllini on the Peloponnese mainland go either to Argostóli (2¾hrs) or Póros (1½hrs), a little east-coast port growing into a resort. The road from Argostóli to Póros, 28 miles (45km) along the south coast is not so dramatic as those northwards, but has slopes thick with olives and cypresses and sea views.

You pass through neat modern-looking villages rebuilt after the earthquake. At one of these, Metaxáta, Byron wrote much of his satirical poem *Don Juan.* Póros is still being rebuilt after the earthquake damage and though not pretty is friendly, with genuine tavernas, a few small hotels and a long shingle beach with clear aquamarine seas. The countryside is rich in spring with wild flowers, lemon trees and olives. The big restaurant of the Hotel Hercules has a terrace and dining room overlooking the bay from a rock. There are little restaurants in the harbour and tavernas over the hill beside the beach. There is a small disco, but 'nightlife' is really confined to eating, drinking and chatting. Almost everything shuts down out of season.

◆
SKÁLA

Five miles (8km) south of Póros is the village of Skála with a stretch of golden sand enormous by Greek standards, almost undeveloped but with a few tavernas, a store and two bars. A few villas let rooms, so does the Miabeli taverna.

◆
SÁMI

The road from Argostóli to Sámi, another small port on the east coast, is truly dramatic, climbing through the mountains past Mount Aínos (5,312ft, 1,619m). On fine days there are views to Zákynthos, Kyllini's Venetian castle, mainland mountains and the isles of Itháki (Ithaca) and Lefkáda. An energetic walk to a hut at 3,937 feet (1,200m) leads on through the historic Kefallonian firs to Megalos Soros, another 985 feet (300m) up. Sámi (the ancient capital Same of Homer's days, 15½ miles, 25km, from Argostóli) was devastated by the 1953 earthquake and much of it is still prefabricated. The bay is attractive. It is the port for Ithaca ferries and has a daily ferry from mainland Patras (4hrs) which itself is linked to Venice, Ancona and Brindisi.

◆◆◆
CAVES

Near to Sámi are several strange caves. Spílaio Drogkaráti has impressively-lit, many-coloured stalactites and stalagmites and its acoustics are so good that concerts are held in it.

Limni Melissani ('Purple Cave') a mile (2km) north on the road towards the charming fishing port of Agía Effimía, has a deep circular bowl 250 feet (75m) round, with a lake at the bottom which changes colour from blue to purple with changing light. Once it was believed to be bottomless and unreachable. An underground cavern known to the ancient Greeks was found in the 1960s and opened up as a route to the lake. With a guide you can take a boat on it.

The attractive port of Sámi is used by ferries as well as fishing boats

*There is a breath-taking view from
the top of the hillside overlooking
Ásos Bay*

◆◆◆
NORTHERN KEFALLONIÁ

For the superb climbing drive
northwards from Argostóli it is
worth hiring a taxi for the day.
At the pretty village of Divaráta
there is a hair-raising drive
down a track to the beach, but
there is a lovely view down
there and another dazzling view
as the road meets the coast.
Look down the cliffs to the
beach and blue sea of Kólpos
Mýrtou (Myrtos Bay). The
mountain scenery becomes
more dramatic towards the
little fishing town of Ásos, 18½
miles (30km) from Argostóli,
where you will find the most

beautiful scene of all. From the
white quayside, red-roofed
white houses spread up a
hillside and onto a strip of land
cutting into the sea to join a tiny
peninsula – a rugged hill,
terraced fields and olive groves
capped by a 16th-century
Venetian fortress, built as
defence against Turkish pirates.
The views are superb.

North from Ásos round the north
tip of the isle you pass woods of
cypresses and deserted bays to
reach the fishing village of
Fiskárdo. Little touched by the
earthquake, it shows you what
Kefalloniá was like before the
1953 disaster and is the most
delightful place on the island.
Ask about rooms to rent at the
village shop on the tiny square
where buses arrive, or at the
quayside Captain's Cabin
taverna, where the owner and
his wife speak English. You will
get good fish in the Thendrinos
restaurant and the Nicholas
taverna, and lobster, at a price,
at Hirodotos taverna. Fiskárdo *is*
a bit pricey.

Festivals

Carnival is held at Argostóli on
the last Sunday and Monday
before Lent. 15 May is the
Festival of the Radicals
(celebrating union with Greece)
in Argostóli.

Accommodation

Xenia, (tel: 0671-22233), is the
best hotel in Argostóli, B-class.
Cephalonia Star Hotel, 50
Metaxa Street, almost opposite
the ferry, is convenient (tel:
0671-23180/3).
The best hotels are found at the
beaches. Lássi: **Mediterranée**,
A-grade, on its private beach,

informal atmosphere; all rooms with private WC and shower; seawater pool; restaurant, soundproofed disco – a good family hotel (tel: 0671-28761/3). Platýs Gialós: **Princess**, B-class, (tel: 0671-25591**)**.
Sámi: **Ionion**, 5 Horofylakis, near ferry (tel: 0674-22035). Platia Kyprou: **Kyma** (in the main square), D-grade and simple (tel: 0674-22064).
Póros: **Hercules Hotel**, B-class pension (tel: 0674-72351), on rocks between the ferry harbour and town square, small pebble beach. **Hotel Kefalos**, in town square, all rooms with WC, shower, balcony (tel: 0674-72139-41). Fiskárdo: **Panormos Pension**, B-class; book ahead (tel: 0674-51340). Lixoúri: **Hotel Summery**, C-grade; best in town (tel: 0671-91771).

Restaurants
Robola, made on the island, is one of the best white wines in Greece.
In Argostóli, the **Argostóli** restaurant next to the Rex cinema serves good cheap Greek food. **Taverna Demosthenes** just off the square is friendly, serves good fresh dishes. **Kefalos** restaurant on left side of the square is recommended for cheap meals; **Kanaria**, top left of the square, for good slightly dearer meals. The **Port of Cephalos** along the waterfront serves the best food and is 'fashionable'.

General Information
Population: 28,000
Area: 301⅓sq miles (781sq km)
Tourist Office: tel: 0671-22248.
Tourist Police: Cruise liner quay (tel: 0671-22200).
Harbour Police: tel: 0671-22224.

How to Get There
Air: There are flights daily from Athens; from Zákynthos 2–3 times a week. Some charters fly direct from other European countries.
Ferries: from Kyllini (Peloponnese) 2 daily to Póros (1½hrs) or Argostóli (2¾hrs). Some boats go to Zákynthos in summer. From Sámi to Patras (mainland) daily in summer; Sámi to Itháki daily (1hr); from Sámi or Fiskárdo to Corfu (one a week from each). In summer a caique goes from Fiskárdo to the isle of Lefkáda (50mins).
Coach: From Athens via Patras.

ITHÁKI (ITHACA)
Only a rocky 17 miles long and 4 miles wide (27 x 6.5km), Itháki is famous as the home of Odysseus, hero of Homer's *Odyssey*. A simple place with friendly people, it attracts few tourists although it is only 1¼ miles (2km) from Kefalloniá at its nearest point and now has a modern road almost from top to bottom and another round much of the coast. Most visitors come for the day and are gone by 18.00hrs, but yachts stay longer.

◆◆
ITHÁKI TOWN
Itháki Town (also sometimes called Vathí), port and capital, was where Odysseus was dumped, to sleep after his 20 years' adventurous journey from the Siege of Troy. It is hidden in a deep long inlet like a fjord, past a high headland,

and is almost surrounded by green conical hills. Houses joined by steep steps cling to the slopes. There is a small archaeological museum.

The isle is shaped like two bulges joined by a narrow strip half a mile (800m) wide. At this narrow point is Mount Aetós (Eagle), where eagles still nest. A short walk west of Itháki Town takes you to Marmarospiliá (Cave of the Nymphs), which Odysseus visited incognito immediately on his return, to hide gifts brought from Corfu. Surrounded by cypress trees, the cave has a narrow entrance to a 50-foot (15m) chamber, with a hole in the roof cut to let out the smoke of sacrificial fires, called 'The Entrance of the Gods'. The caves are open in high summer. Otherwise apply at the town hall in Itháki Town for the keys.

A rewarding signposted walk of 3 miles (5km) south from Itháki Town, past a clifftop, leads to Arethusa's Fountain. Poor Arethusa was a nymph who cried so much when her son died that she turned into a fountain. Homer's story says that here Odysseus was recognised by his faithful old dog, though he had been away 20 years.

◆
STAVRÓS

Odysseus's city is now said to be in the north at Stavrós, 10½ miles (17km) from Itháki Town. It is little more than a street and a square, half-filled with the chairs and tables of a genuine, simple taverna. Near by at Polis Bay is a quay used by fishing boats, and from here some tourist boats go to Fiskárdo on Kefalloniá.

FRÍKES

The charming fishing village of Fríkes runs along an attractive valley to a little square and port, with a hotel and tavernas. There is a sailing centre, and boats go to Itháki Town and also, if you are lucky, to Vasilikí on Lefkáda. On a hillside 2½ miles (4km) away, overlooking its port, is the prettiest village on Itháki, Kióni. There are food shops, several tavernas and very small beaches. A good hideaway, Fríkes is 12½ miles (20km) across the island from Itháki Town.

Accommodation

The best and most modern hotel in Itháki Town is the **Mendor** (B-grade), Georg Drakouli Street, out of town centre, open only in summer (tel: 0674-32433). The alternative is the C-class **Odysseus** (tel: 0674-32381).

Restaurants

The main square of Itháki Town has a row of pavement taverna-cafés. The best is **Penelope**, with a downstairs bar and upstairs restaurant offering varied dishes. Best food in town is at a taverna called simply **Taverna**, offering charcoal-grilled meat, fish, and *souvlakia*, and Greek dishes simmering on the stove. You can tell it is good, because it is a meeting place for locals. It is behind the town hall opposite the popular **Pension Enoikiazomena** (old rooms; cheap).

General Information

Population: 3,600
Area: 37sq miles (96sq km)
Tourist Office & Tourist Police:
in police station (tel: 0674-
32205).
Harbour Police: tel: 0674-31206.
Also house on jetty: (tel: 0674-
32909).
Buses are scarce. Roads can be
rough for scooters. Taxis are
reasonably priced.

How to Get There

Ferries: daily from Itháki Town
to Sámi on Kefalloniá (1hr) and
on to Patras (mainland, 5hrs).
Every other day to Paxoí and
Corfu. Daily to Astakos on the
mainland (1¾hrs). In summer
there are boats from Stavrós to
Fiskárdo (Kefalloniá) and from
Frikes to Vasilikí (Lefkáda).
Coach: From Athens via Patras.

LEFKÁDA (LEVKAS)

The bus direct from Athens
does not have to board a ferry
to reach Lefkáda, for the island
is joined to the province of
Aetolia-Akarnania on the
mainland by a causeway with a
wide road. It became an island
in 540 BC when Corinthian
colonists cut a canal, which was
widened by the Venetians. You
can also cross by a chain-ferry.

◆◆
LEFKÁDA TOWN

Lefkáda suffered from an
earthquake in 1948 when
Greece was too poor for much
rebuilding. So some upper
storeys of buildings are still of
boarding and corrugated iron.
But there are old stone
churches with solid bell towers
and tall houses with Turkish
wooden balconies and with
flowers and plants as covering,
so there is no hint of shanty-
town. The big quay is a yacht-
chartering centre. There is the
usual archaeological museum,
an icon museum in the public
library, a folklore museum and
the Lefkáda Sound Museum
(29 Kalkari Street) founded by a
local collector with old
gramophones sent over by

*Lefkáda is a quiet little place, with
an abundance of good produce*

relatives from the US, records of Greek songs from the 1920s and some 1914 recordings. The east coast is dotted with pleasant villages. Vliho, in a fjord-like bay lined with mountains, is delightfully quiet. Nydrí is a lovely fishing port with fine views of a bay with tiny islands. Sailing flotillas call. There are rooms to let in villas and tavernas. Ferries go from Nydrí to the little green isle of Meganísi (tranquil, with some rooms in the three villages). South from Nydrí is a delightful little fishing port, Sývota, with grass to the water's edge. Buses go twice a day from Lefkáda Town to Kalamítsi on the west coast, which has the best beach, but you must tackle a steep track of hairpin bends, potholes and boulders to reach the sea.

VASILIKÍ

Buses serve several towns and villages but only twice a day, except to Nydrí and the equally attractive fishing village of Vasilikí. It is on the south coast about 24 miles (38km) from Lefkáda. There is a board-sailing school in Vasilikí at Hotel Lefkatas. From here caiques sail to several nearby islands, including Kefalloniá. From Vasilikí you can go by caique or by road (rough) via Komylió to Cape (Akra) Doukáto – the original Lover's Leap. From here the poet Sappho, from Lesbos, leapt to her death for love of a handsome boatman. The priests from Apollo's temple made the jump successfully as part of their ritual. Rumour has it that they used a net.

Festivals

International Folklore Festival, last two weeks of August.

Accommodation

Behind the main quay of Lefkáda port are three B-class, fairly good hotels, with bedrooms with WC and shower: **Xenia Lefkáda**, overlooking canal (tel:(0645-24762/3); **Niricos**, Agía Mavra (tel: 0645-24132); **Lefkáda**, 2 Panagou Street (tel: 0645-23916/8). Others include **Santa Mavra** in the small square, Odos Darfeld, off the high street behind the lagoon, C-class (tel: 0645-22342)

Restaurants

Lefkáda specialises in salads made with fried marinated fish. Prices rise in places where flotilla yachts call. Lefkáda Town: **Lighthouse** taverna (in alley opposite the church) has excellent food. Other good tavernas are **Romantica** (Ioan Mala – main street) and **Pete's** (on the square behind the lagoon). Vasilikí: **Taverna Ionian** opposite Post Office (simple, cheap). Nydrí: good tavernas along the waterfront.

General Information

Population: 24,000
Area: 114sq miles (295sq km).
Tourist Police: tel: 0645-22346.

How to Get There

Air: Flights to Aktion from Athens, plus summer charters.
Ferries: Chain-ferry from Préveza to Aktion beside causeway. Summer caiques go from Vasilikí to Itháki Town and Fiskárdo (Kefalloniá).
Coaches: Athens–Aktion, then across the causeway (7hrs).

DODECANESE

KÁRPATHOS

Kárpathos changes more slowly than any other of the 12 Dodecanese Islands. There are not enough roads or rooms to lure many tourists, and only a few buses, running in summer; use taxis. Not until 1979 was there a road linking the fertile south and the mountainous north, and many people still go between them by boat. Now, as well as an air link with Rhodes and Crete using very small planes (15-seaters), charter planes land from Britain and elsewhere in Europe. A few visitors are emigrants from the US returning to see families or to find an island girl to marry. The Pan Karpathian Society of America symbolises a tight community keeping alive the island's culture, publishing a magazine and even choosing an annual 'Miss Kárpathos'.

Because of its relative isolation from other islands, Kárpathos remained very conservative and is one of the few islands where some people in remoter villages – notably Ólympos, in the north of the island – still wear traditional costume. Until the road was finally built along the steep and narrow mountain ridge which connects the northern and southern parts of the island, the northern villages could be reached only by sea.

◆◆
KÁRPATHOS TOWN

Ferries call at the thriving little port of Kárpathos, also known as Pigádia, in the south, and at Diafáni in the north. Kárpathos, in a bay where mountains meet sea, has quite a number of

Vrontis Bay, Kárpathos

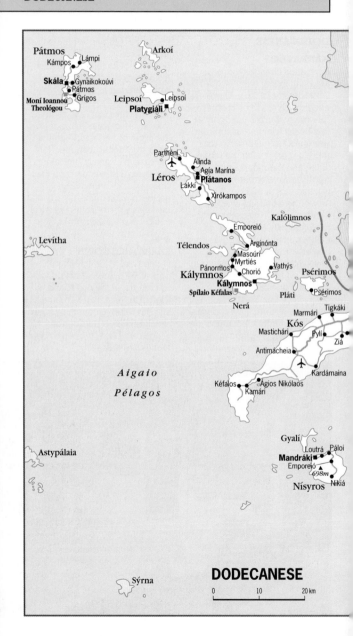

Pátmos
Kámpos · Lámpi
Skála · Gynaikokoúvi
· Pátmos
Moní Ioannoú · Grigos
Theológou

Arkoí

Leipsoí · Leipsoí
Platygiáli ■

Parthéni ✈
Alinda
Agía Marína
Plátanos ■
Léros
Lákkí
Xirókampos

Kalólimnos

Levítha

Emporeió
Arginónta
Télendos · Masoúri
Myrtiés
Pánormos · Chorió · Vathýs
Kálymnos
Kálymnos ■
Spílaio Kéfalas
Nerá
Pláti

Psérimos
· Psérimos

Marmári
Tigkáki
Kós
Mastichári · Pyli
Ziá
Antimácheia ·
✈
Kardámaina

Aigaio
Pélagos
Kéfalos · Ágios Nikólaos
Kamári

Astypálaia

Gyalí
Loutrá · Páloi
Mandráki ■ ·
Emporeió ·
▲ 698m
Nikiá
Nísyros

DODECANESE
0   10   20 km

Sýrna

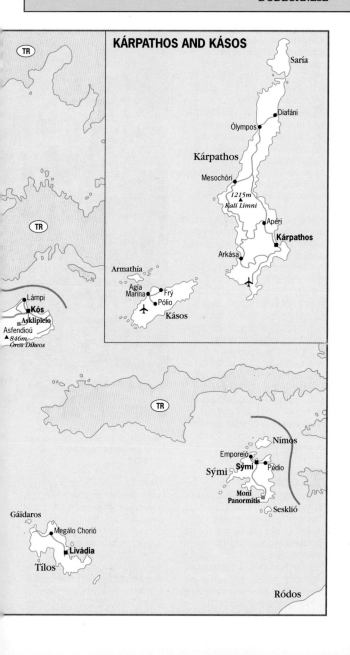

KÁRPATHOS AND KÁSOS

Saría

TR

Diafáni

Ólympos

Kárpathos

Mesochóri

▲ 1215m
Kalí Límni

Apéri

Kárpathos

TR

Arkása

Armathía

Lámpi

Ágia Marina

Frý

Kós

Pólio

Asklipíelo

Kásos

Asfendioú

▲ 846m
Óros Díkeos

TR

Nímos

Emporeió

Sými

Sými

Pédio

Moni Panormítis

Sesklió

Gáïdaros

Megálo Chorió

Livádia

Tílos

Ródos

DODECANESE

small hotels, pensions and rooms and is building more. A road leads from here to the small beach resort of Ammopi, with a string of small beaches, tavernas and rooms.

There are several quiet beaches up the east coast, accessible by land or by boat. Apella is in a dramatic setting of rugged rock formations, steep gorges and huge boulders left by the Titans of Greek legend. These giants tore lumps off the mountain to throw at each other. Ágios Nikólaos, a fishing village further north, has a few rooms and a taverna owned by a fisherman, whose wife cooks the catch.

A road crosses the isle to Finiki (harbour of Arkása), a large fishing village and caique port, with a very good fish taverna. Just south are relics of ancient Arkása, on a clifftop. Some good Byzantine mosaics remain, though the Italians took most to Rhodes. A rough road up the west coast from Finiki leads to Lefkos, with a white sand beach, shading pines, a small hotel and tavernas. Boats go from Kárpathos Town to the nearby island of Kásos, where there are fine walks and solitude.

You have to be fit to live in – or visit – the awe-inspiring town of Ólympos

◆◆◆
ÓLYMPOS

The road to Ólympos in the north, 37 miles (60km) from Kárpathos Town, is reasonable as far as Apéri, the old capital, which has a cathedral containing an icon credited with several miracles. Then it deteriorates, but around the scary corners you see some fine sea and mountain views that make Ólympos beautiful. It is clamped to a mountain ridge, its white, blue and beige houses, many with decorative balconies, are terraced upwards and joined by alleys and donkey steps. No car can get past the first taverna. A line of windmills runs down the edge. The mountain dives from the village to the sea on one side, steps down by cultivated terraces to a fertile valley on the other. There is no bus from Kárpathos to Ólympos, so share a taxi.

Alternatively, you can take a boat to the northern port of Diafáni, about 25 miles (40km) up the coast, and a shorter taxi or minibus ride from there on a track-road.

◆
DIAFÁNI
This is a small, pleasant resort with a beach backed by pine woods, and a few rooms and tavernas. The Mayflower Hotel has six rooms and a good fish restaurant. A boat goes on Sundays to the tiny isle of Sariá, deserted except for summer shepherds. A hard walk leads to Ta Palatia (the Palaces), small, stone domed houses, once a pirate base.

Accommodation
Possirama Bay, (tel: 0245-22916), class-A apartments. Karpáthos: **Porfyris**, C-class, clean, close to beach; good meals (tel: 0245-22294).

Restaurants
Karpáthos: **George's**, below the bank, has fine seafood. Ólympos: **Artemis Pension** has excellent fish dishes.

General Information
Population: 6,500
Area: 117sq miles (304sq km)
227 nautical miles from Piréas.
Tourist Police: tel: 0245-22218.

How to Get There
Air: There are flights twice daily from Rhodes (40mins), several a week from Crete (Siteía) (45mins) and three times a week from Kásos.
Ferries: 4 times a week from Piréas (23hrs); twice a week from Rhodes (7½hrs), Kásos, Crete and Halki.

Link with the Past
There are some who believe that the people of Ólympos are descended from Dorian Greeks of 3,000 years ago. They use a language, it seems, seen otherwise today only in the works of Homer.
Unmarried girls wear old gold jewellery, some made from gold foreign coins sent home by fathers working abroad. Once they are married, they put the gold away to pass to their daughters.

DODECANESE

SÝMI ✓

Sými is so attractively serene that people on day excursions from Rhodes or Kós sometimes jump ship and stay for days. Wily visitors take the island's only bus, or walk through fields of oregano, to the pebbly beach at Pédio, which has an hotel and tavernas, and where they also repair caiques.

You sail into the harbour past steep cliffs sheer to the sea. Rounding a point you see the harbour like a fjord of deep blue, ending in the town of white and ochre houses with red roofs. Alongside the boats are neo-classical houses built last century from the profits of shipbuilding and sponge-diving. These were empty and crumbling until recently. Now many are being restored, even to their mosaic courtyards. Sými dare not build many hotels or encourage too

many visitors to stay because of a water shortage, so when the flotilla of excursion boats from Rhodes leaves in late afternoon, the port reverts to tranquillity; the tavernas at night are packed with as many locals eating, drinking and talking as visitors. By day, the harbour quay is constantly busy, with boats landing fish, vegetables from Rhodes, and black sponges to be washed and beaten clean. Caiques ply, taking visitors to remote beaches of the island, to Nímos, the isle of shepherds to the north, where visitors can swim, fish and walk, or to fertile Sesklió southward, owned by the monks of Moní Panormítis. Boat-building made Sými prosperous. When the Knights of St John were there they let Symians go their own way so

Sými, tiny and delightfully serene, is a real 'get away from it all' island

long as they built them fast solid ships. The Turks so liked the Symian *skaphes*, fast-sailing courier boats, that they allowed Symians to own land on the shores of Turkey, and gave them the right to dive for sponges in any Turkish-controlled waters in return for sponges for the ladies of Sultan Suleiman's harem.

Sými's depression started when the Italians took the Dodecanese in 1912 and cut off the Symians from their Turkish trade. The population dropped from 20,000 to 2,200 as the young emigrated. Tourism and fishing have restored prosperity.

The port is two towns: the harbour area, Ghialos, joined by Kali Strata, a 'high street' of 357 steps, to Chóra, the high town, 275 more steps lead to a monastery. Mules and donkeys carry most things – even building materials. It is a long way round by the bus road. You must walk or take a truck-ride into the interior and mountains where pine and cypress flourish. A road now runs to Moní Panormítis (Panormítis monastery), on a horseshoe bay 9 miles (5km) south. There are no buses, but some excursions, and excursion boats from Rhodes to Ghialos call here. The building is mostly 18th century, with a mock baroque bell tower of 1905. The chapel has a remarkable carved icon, and the museum has beautiful carved model ships and little bottles thrown out by passing sailors to drift ashore with money for the monastery. It has a restaurant, café, food shop and cells where you can stay. Make a donation when you leave.

Accommodation
It is advisable to pre-book rooms in high summer. **Aliki**, A-class, is a lovely old house (tel: 0241-71665); booking essential. **Dorian**, another old house, costs much the same (tel: 0241-71181). **Nireus** (next door to Aliki) is modern bungalow style, B-class (tel: 0241-71386). For monastery accommodation (200 cell-like rooms), phone 0241-71354.

Restaurants
Shrimps and lobsters are especially good on Sými. *Fragosyko*, a local version of Turkish Delight made from figs, is worth trying. **Les Katerinettes** (also a pension) is one of the best places to eat near the harbour, but most tavernas are worth trying. **George's**, in the Chóra, has good views.

General Information
Population: 2,200
Area: 20⅓sq miles (53sq km)
230 nautical miles from Piréas.
Tourist Police: tel: 0241-71111.

How to Get There
Ferries: From Rhodes daily in summer, fewer in winter (2hrs); 1 or 2 a week from Piréas, Astypálaia, Amorgós, Kálymnos, Kós, Léros, Nísyros, Páros, Pátmos, Sámos and Tílos.

KÓS
Kós has joined Corfu, Crete and Rhodes as one of the big tourist isles of Greece. The old lazy waterfront of Kós Town now seethes with people walking, cycling, or eating and drinking at the pavement taverna tables, and with coaches, taxis and bicycles.

Flotilla yachts and more luxurious craft slap against the fishing boats at the quayside. Side roads are packed with more bars and restaurants, shops selling clothes, leather goods and liquor at Kós's duty-free prices, and travel agents offering excursions to other isles. Round the harbour towards Lámpi new roads are thick with small modern hotels and apartment blocks, shops and restaurants. The ghosts of the Knights of St John who built the formidable medieval castle at the harbour's end must look in wonder at the noisy hydrofoils making for other isles, tourists parascending over the beach and girls sunbathing topless. And across the island Kardámaina has developed in a few years from a fishing port with fish tavernas on its quay into a lively little resort with hotels, small apartment blocks, crowded tavernas and a beach full of browning bodies. There are noisy water-scooters, too, and dozens of throbbing discos and dance clubs. But somehow it retains much of its fishing port atmosphere. And the farming villages of the interior and remoter beaches of Kós, reached by mule track, bear no relation to the scene in Kós Town. Kós has many good roads, safe for experienced scooter drivers. There are fairly good bus services in summer, plenty of taxis, and cars for hire. Many visitors hire bicycles.

◆◆
KÓS TOWN
The town is a jolly place, with infectious happiness and relaxation. Even its crumbling

Italian mansions have a certain decadent charm. And the fishermen still sell their catch on the quay to passers-by. It is surprising how Kós has remained so Greek, despite being occupied from 197 BC, when the Romans took over, until 1945 when the British Army freed it from the Germans who had taken it in 1943 from the Italians. Under Mussolini all education was in Italian and farms were given to Italian immigrants, turning local Greek farmers into farm workers.
In the town, ancient Greek ruins are scattered around so liberally that locals treat them casually. The well-restored amphitheatre is sometimes used as an open-air theatre. The Archaeological Museum has mosaics from the 3rd century AD and statues, including Hermes with a dog (open: 08.30–15.00hrs; closed: Mondays). Apart from the 15th-century Knights' castle, there are interesting old Turkish mosques. But the important site is truly Greek. Hippocrates, 'Father of Modern Medicine', was born here about 460 BC. He preached diagnosis by observation and treatment by baths and diet. (The priests believed in magical cures.) A huge old twisted plane tree by the castle is where he is supposed to have taught his pupils. In fact, it is a mere 600 years old.

◆◆
THE ASKLIPIEÍO
Two and a half miles (4km) south of Kós Town is the Asklipiéio, built in the 4th century BC, after Hippocrates died. It is a shrine to the healing god Aesculapius

whose priests believed that baths in a lovely setting were good for body and soul. Snakes were their symbol and have remained a medical symbol. The temple drew people suffering with problems from baldness to blindness. The site is set on four levels, once graced by altars and statues, near springs with iron content – the fountain of Pan.

◆◆
LÁMPI

The beach north of the town has many tavernas and at Lámpi, 4¼ miles (7km) north is the primitive-looking taverna Faros, which serves some of the best taverna food in the Greek Isles. Choose from raw fresh fish, meat on the slab and copper pots on the cooker. A new B-class hotel at Lámpi, the little Cosmopolitan (tel: 0242-23411/5) is very friendly.

OTHER BEACHES

A sand beach along the north coast, Tigkáki (8¾ miles/14km) from Kós Town), with good fish tavernas and a number of package-tour hotels, has fine sand but winds. The fishing village of Marmári, 10 miles (16km) from Kós, has a few hotels and a nearby beach. Mastichári, a fishing village with a shaded beach 15½ miles (25km) from Kós Town, is pleasant. Boats go from here to the isles of Psérimos and Kálymnos. Kéfalos, 26¾ miles (43km) from Kós, just inland from the east coast, has a ruined Knights' castle with a medieval legend of a dragon living in a cave, and the ruins of Astypálaia, ancient capital of the island. A beach half a mile (1km) away at

Kós Town: the tree forming part of the background is the famous Hippocrates Tree. Kós Town is described on page 74

Kamári has a fishing boat quay, a taverna and a rocky islet, Ágios Nikólaos, with a fishermen's chapel. Tavernas along the bay lead to a Club Mediterranée with watersports in magnificently blue clear sea and nude sunbathing on the rocks. Then begins Paradissos Bay (Almiros) with good sands but no shade. The sea is warm and slightly bubbly from the volcanic seabed. Kardámaina up the coast and 18 miles (29km) from Kós Town, is still a superb place for tasting fish, but is not a good centre for inter-island touring. Boats and hydrofoils nearly all go from Kós Town before the buses from Kardámaina arrive, so taxis are often necessary from here.

INLAND VILLAGES
Pylí, 10½ miles (17km) southwest of Kós Town, is a mountain village with superb views to the sea. A 2½-mile (4km) path leads to the remains of a Byzantine castle. Asfendioú, on the slopes of Óros (Mount) Díkeos, 9 miles (14km) from Kós Town, is really five hamlets. Zía is beautiful, with steep white alleys, courtyards where they bake bread, and many flowers. Excursion coaches call in during the day, and in the evening to see the sunset, watch Greek dancing and taste the wine. This is a wine district. Some renovated houses are let to visitors (ask the Tourist Office in Kós Town for bookings – (0242-24400). May and September are good months for Kós, but then there are fewer boats to other islands than during the summer season.

Accommodation
Virtually all hotels on the island are block-booked by British, German and Scandinavian tour companies throughout the summer and it is hard to find accommodation independently. The most luxurious hotel is the **Ramira Beach** outside Kós Town in Psalidí, A-class (tel: 0242-22891/4). **Astron**, near the harbour (B-class), is modern, with good views from the rooftop garden (tel: 0242-23705/7). Kardámaina: **Norida Beach** complex is 'international';

A-class (tel: 0242-91231/2). **Stelios** on the main square is more fun, but book ahead (tel: 0242-91293). Between Kardámaina and Kéfalos, is the A-class **Lakitira** (tel: 0242-91115).

Restaurants
Eat in very Greek tavernas, as some restaurants serve bland 'international' food. Tavernas in Kós Town are mostly popular and a little pricey. **Limani** on the waterfront is fashionable and offers good Greek food. The **Bristol Taverna's Garden** restaurant is popular and the Bristol hotel is a small, clean bed and breakfast pension (tel: 0242) 22865.

General Information
Population: 21,350
Area: 112sq miles (290sq km)
192 nautical miles from Piréas.
Tourist Office: tel: 0242-24400.
Tourist Police: next door to Tourist Office (tel: 0242-24444).
Harbour Police: tel: 0242-28527.

How to Get There
Air: There are charters from several European capitals. Flights from Athens arrive 1–3 times a day, from Rhodes most days, and from Mýkonos four times a week in July and August. **Ferries**: daily from Piréas (14hrs), Pátmos, Léros, Kálymnos and Rhodes; 2–3 a week from Nísyros, Tílos and Sými. There are irregular services to Chíos, Lésvos, Límnos, Crete, Santoríni and Mílos, and dozens of excursions in summer. **Hydrofoils**: irregular service June to September from Rhodes, Pátmos, Sámos and Léros.

A general view of the little port of Myrtiés, across Kálymnos

KÁLYMNOS and LÉROS

Kálymnos is an island of deep blue, fjord-like bays and bare white limestone hills, pocked with caves and dotted with green valley-deltas of cultivation where the mountains meet the sea. With so little fertile land, islanders have (until the advent of tourism) been dependent on the sea, and Kálymnos's sponge-divers ranged as far as the North African coast, Florida and even Cuba. These days the ubiquitous sponges are more likely to have been hauled up by local divers.

Prosperous from the 19th-century sponge trade, Kálymnos Town, the island's capital. is a charmingly cluttered harbour surrounded by doll's-house-like mansions and cafés patronised by elderly traders and captains, many of them retired from sponge-fishing in Florida or the Bahamas. Kálymnos is twinned with Tarpon Springs in Florida, which was founded by expatriate Kalymniot sponge-divers and their families, many of whom return to Kálymnos for the traditional Easter festival, when the island celebrates for a week with music, dancing in local costume, eating and drinking. In the past, this was when the sponge boats left to a peal of church bells, returning with their sponges for more celebrations in October. Then, the Kalymniot divers used primitive weighted diving suits and their air was pumped to them through a hose. These days, tourism offers a less risky and more profitable living.

◆◆
CHORIÓ (KÁLYMNOS TOWN)

The harbour here is packed with ships, and hotels and tavernas stretch round the harbour bay to the little beach.

In this scrum are some fine works of art Agía Ekaterini Church on the harbour has lovely decorations in gold, blue and brown, and superb icons. Local sculptors Michail Kokkinos and his daughter Irene have adorned the town with statues. Two works are *Winged Victory* in Liberty Square, and *Poseidon* by the Olympic Hotel.

The island, which looks barren and rocky as you approach, has hidden fertile valleys of figs, mandarins, lemons and vines. One such valley leads to the delightful fishing hamlet of Vathýs, with its tiny harbour and two tavernas at the end of a long fjord, 7½ miles (12km) from Kálymnos Town. Buses are infrequent, it is best to share taxis on Kálymnos.

BEACHES

Across the island are the sandy beaches: Pánormos, Myrtiés, from where boats go to Télendos, Masoúri and Emporeió. The north is deserted.

◆◆◆
LÉROS

Léros is unspectacular and off the beaten tourism track, though it has found favour with some tour operators in search of new destinations to offer. It was Italy's naval base during the Italian occupation of the Dodecanese, and some odd Italian architecture remains. There are few good beaches, but it has peace and quiet to recommend it.

Accommodation

Xenon Angelou, (tel: (0247) 22514) is a restored mansion-hotel, A-class, at Lakkí, the spectacular natural harbour.

Restaurants

Most tavernas are by beaches and around the Kálymnos Town harbour – **Stelios Restaurant** is still the most popular here. In Myrtiés, the **Myrtiés** has a veranda with harbour views.

General Information

Population: 14,300
Area: 43sq miles (111sq km)
183 nautical miles from Piréas.
Tourist Office & Tourist Police: Kálymnos Town (tel: 0243-22100).

How to Get There

Air: Connections from Athens.
Ferries: From Piréas via Léros (12hrs), Kós (1hr) and Rhodes 4–6 times a week; from Pátmos and Psérimos 3 times a week. Léros can also be reached by hydrofoil in summer from Kós, Rhodes, Pátmos and Sámos.

PÁTMOS ✓

Pátmos is a holy isle and is invaded in summer by hordes of visitors and day-trippers. Here the apostle John heard the voice of God through cracks in the ceiling of a cave, and dictated to his disciple Prochorus the prophetic poem the *Apocalypse*, which we call *Revelations*.

◆◆
CHÓRA (PÁTMOS TOWN)

Visitors come to see the cave, now a chapel, and to visit Moní Ioannis Theológos (Monastery of St John the Divine), founded in 1088 by St Christodoulos, on a hill 2¾ miles (4km) south of the port of Skála. Buses go up the hill, but the hour's hard walk is rewarding for its superb views. The monastery was fortified against pirates so successfully that it has survived all those centuries of raids and invasions. It is still one of the richest religious houses in the world. Thirteenth-century frescoes decorate the chapels. The library with thousands of rare old books is the most prized building, but you need the abbot's permission to see them. Scholars have 'borrowed' many priceless items over the centuries and they are now in national libraries in France, Germany and England. Zoodochos Pigi convent (1607), accepts visitors and has good frescoes and icons. Superb 17th-century mansions built by wealthy shipping magnates line twisting narrow streets, but they are usually shuttered and you cannot see their courtyards. They are used now by rich Athenians as holiday homes.

◆◆
SKÁLA

Skála is a pleasant little town with a busy square and small hotels and tavernas, calmer when the day visitors have gone. Two discos are discreet. Pátmos has 14 miles (22.5km) of roads, and bus services are not bad, but walking is better. Motorcycles are useful. Still better is to go on a caique trip.

Accommodation

Skála: **Patmion**, on the waterfront, B-class (tel: 0247-31313). **Chris**, waterfront, C-class (tel: 0247-31001). Grikou: **Xenia**, B-class (tel: 0247-31219). **Flisvos**, D-class, cheap (tel: 0247-31380).

Restaurants

Victor Gouras' **Patmian House** in a Chóra mansion serves superb

food, but is pricey. There are good fish restaurants in Skála.

General Information

Population: 2,500
Area: 13sq miles (34sq km)
163 nautical miles from Piréas.
Police: harbour (tel: 0247-31303).

How to Get There

Ferries: From Piréas (8hrs) Rhodes, Kós, Kálymnos and Léros 6 days a week; from Sámos 3 times a week; from Ikaría once or twice weekly; May to September. Weekly Dodecanese island boat; daily summer.caique to Leipsoí. **Hydrofoils**: in summer from Kós and Rhodes 3 times a week; Léros twice weekly.

One of the medieval treasures in the Monastery of St John on Pátmos

NORTH SPORADES AND NORTH AEGEAN

SÁMOS ✓

A pretty island only 1¾ miles
(3km) from the Turkish coast,
Sámos was one of the first to
accept charter holiday flights
and is very popular with
German, Italian and Austrian
package tourists. Pythagóreio,
Kokkári and Órmos are
crowded small resorts. The
island's greenery comes from
natural springs, but you will find
most of its beauty inland,
especially in the south, where
there are pine woods, figs, olive
groves and many vineyards.
Samian wine has been famous
through history. The sweet red
is easy to get. Most of the dry
white goes to Athens. Parts of
the rocky north coast are
inaccessible. Summer bus
services are good but stop in
the early evening.

◆◆
VATHÍ (SÁMOS TOWN)
The main town and Piréas ferry
port, set in a U-shaped bay, is
called Vathí, but the deep-port
part is called Sámos Town and
has a fine archaeological
museum. Restoration of elegant
19th-century buildings has
improved its looks. Even the old
part of Vathí on a steep hillside is
still a working town not a tourist
resort, though there are many
pensions available.

◆◆
PYTHAGÓREIO
Rooms are hard to find in the
other, much more attractive, port
of Pythagóreio, 8 miles (13km)
further south. It was called

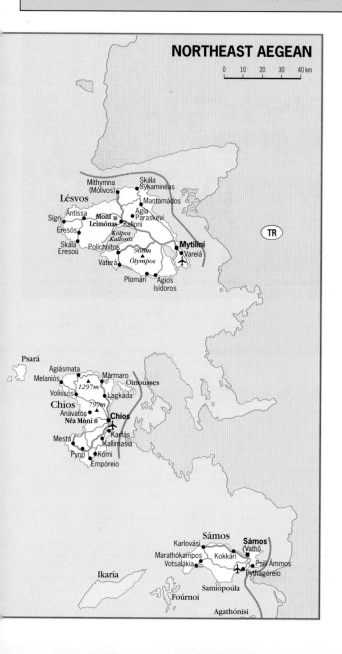

*Tavernas line the waterfront in the
picturesque resort of Kokkári*

Tigani, but was renamed in 1955
in honour of the mathematician
Pythagoras, who was born here
in the 6th century BC. It is still a
fishing port, though smaller
ferries call. The views across the
Mycale Straits to Turkey are
lovely, and the tree- and taverna-
lined harbourside is very
pleasant at night. There is a small
sandy beach and a long pebbly
beach beyond the harbour.
The tyrant-corsair Polycrates
built the great mole on which
the modern town is built, and a
big tunnel nearly a mile (1.5km)
north of the town, incredible for
its time. Nearly 6½ feet (2m) high
and wide, and called Evpalinion
after the engineer, it took
thousands of slaves 15 years to
build. It ran for two-thirds of a
mile (1,000m) through the rock

of Mount Kas, carried water to
the city, and was used as a bolt-
hole when the Persians
attacked. It has collapsed in one
place and unfortunately, it is no
longer possible to explore it.

BEACHES
Once an attractive fishing
village, Kokkári is now a major
holiday resort dominated by
German package tourists. It is
on a bus route 6¼ miles (10km)
from Sámos Town, with a long
pebble beach lined with small
tavernas. Órmos on the south
coast is a delightful old-style
Greek fishing and caique-
building port. Over a headland
about 1¼ miles (2km) away, is
the nicest beach – Votsalákia –
sand and pebble with shade.
There are frequent buses to
Sámos Town, 32 miles (52km)
away. At Psilí Ámmos there is a
super white-sand beach.

Accommodation

Vathí: **Hotel Sámos**, 11 Sophouli Street, facing the harbour, is modern, clean, has rooms with wc, shower, and a restaurant, C-class (tel: 0273-28377/8). **Xenia**, also facing the harbour, is slightly superior, B-class (tel: 0273-27463). Sámos Town: of many pensions, **Ionia**, 5 Manoli Kalomiri, is friendly and reasonable (tel: 0273-28782). Kokkári: **Kokkári Beach Hotel**, right on the shore, is comfortable, C-class (tel: 0273-92263). Pythagóreio: many hotels and pensions, mainly booked by package tours in July/August. **Tarsanas**, on the western sea front, by a pebble beach, is B-class (tel: 0273-61162).

Restaurants

Dionysos restaurant on Sophouli esplanade in Sámos port is clean, rather too neat for a Greek taverna, and serves good, genuinely Greek food. Pythagóreio's waterfront has a big choice of eating places.

General Information

Population: 43,000
Area: 184sq miles (476sq km)
175 nautical miles from Piréas.
Tourist Police: 2 Sahtouri Street (tel: 0273-27980).
Harbour Police: tel: 0273-27318.

How to Get There

Air: Many charter flights go direct from Western European countries in summer. There are 2–3 flights daily from Athens (1hr); from Chíos twice weekly (35mins); from Lésvos 1 or 2 a week (55mins); in summer from Mýkonos 1–4 a week (40mins) also Kós and Thessaloníki.

Ferries: From Piréas, 3–8 a week (12hrs); from Ikaría 3–7 weekly (2½hrs); from Páros 3–4 weekly; from Chíos 2 weekly (4¾hrs); from Lésvos (Mytilíni), Límnos, Kavala (mainland), Kós, Sýros, Léros, Kálymnos, Rhodes, Chálki, Kárpathos, Kásos, Crete, (Siteía, Ágios Nikólaos), Santoríni, Folégandros and Mílos all once a week.

CHÍOS (KHÍOS)

You will not meet many other tourists on Chíos. It is rich and does not go out of its way to encourage visitors. It grew rich on shipping, *mastika* for chewing-gum and varnish, and money brought back from the US by returning emigrants.

◆◆
CHÍOS TOWN

You find high-rise concrete apartments and office blocks in the big port, Chíos Town, and many fast-food hamburger joints and smart plastic bars: more Athenian than Greek-island style. But in the evenings there is the traditional quayside walkabout, with no room for cars or noisy motorcycles until the early hours, when they all rev up at once. The lanes and alleys in the market area are very Greek, too, and there is an old Turkish town within the walls of the fortress. There are bus routes to the south of the isle and buses run frequently in the summer from Chíos Town as far as Pyrgí and Mestá. In the north buses follow the coast to Mármaro. Lagkáda, a delightful fishing village 11 miles (18km) from the port, is at the end of a bay backed by hills thick with pines. Anávatos, 7½ miles (12km) inland, is a medieval village up a steep mountainside to a ruined castle. A nearly vertical cliff hovers over a deep gorge. Three people live in the village. In 1822 the islanders joined the Greek independence fight. Of the 100,000 islanders, the Turks murdered 30,000 and took 45,000 into slavery. The 400 people of Anávatos threw themselves over the cliff to avoid, torture and enslavement. South from Chíos Town is attractive countryside and villages, some, like Sklavia, with Genoese villas and gardens, and houses with watermills. The Genoese ruled Chíos from 1261 to 1566.

On the coast is a very pleasant working fishing port, Kataraktis, with tavernas on its sea front. Further down is Empóreio between hills in a narrow bay. It has good fish tavernas and an unusual and strangely attractive beach of black volcanic pebbles and sand. A track joins it to Kómi, with clean sand and pebble beaches and three tavernas. Another rocky track north leads past a very sandy cove and small-boat harbour, to Ágios Ioannis, a fishing hamlet. Ferries go from Chíos Town to the nearby islands of Oinoússes, where there is a medieval castle, tavernas and hotels, and Psará.

Pyrgí's houses are covered with geometric, black-and-white patterns called xista, *a style of decoration found nowhere else*

♦♦♦
PYRGÍ

Pyrgí, 17 miles (27km) from Chíos, is a superb medieval village, centre of the *mastika*-producing area.

Resin Power

Mastika, or mastic, is a resin tapped from gashes made in lentisk trees. For centuries it was used for chewing-gum to sweeten the breath and for making varnish. Today mastic is used in pharmaceutics, to make a form of ouzo and as a jelly-jam eaten on a spoon. When the Turks took Chíos from Genoa in 1566, the girls of the harems were hooked on chewing-gum, so the mastic farmers of Chíos were given privileges. When the Turks destroyed towns, villages and crops in 1822 they left the mastic villages alone.

The huge close-packed houses of Pyrgí formed a fortified wall against pirates. Their stone walls, doorways and windows are framed with arches, and there are more arches over the narrow streets. On the first floors are small open courtyards with steps up to flat roofs. Balconies are decorated with plants and flowers, and housemartins and swifts nest and swoop along the streets. Most remarkable and beautiful are the graffiti engraved with black sand into the plaster. The attractive 12th-century church of Ágii Apostóli, contains wall paintings by a Cretan artist of 1665. The inhabitants of Pyrgí preserve their traditional customs; many still wear local dress.

♦♦
MESTÁ

Best-preserved of several of these medieval walled villages is Mestá, 7½ miles (12km) northwest of Pyrgí and quieter but with the same delightful Genoese houses. Four have been restored and are small guesthouses run by the National Tourist Organisation of Greece. Several others in a little alley off the main square have been converted into a delightful hotel.

♦♦
NÉA MONÍ

The other great site of Chíos is Néa Moní monastery, 8½ miles (14km) from Chíos Town (buses and excursions). Founded in 1042 when three hermit monks discovered a miraculous icon, it was looted by the Turks in 1822, and the monks all killed. The bell tower and vault collapsed in the 1881 earthquake. Some beautiful mosaics, masterpieces of religious art, have survived. The church is restored and has a 1900s bell tower. Nuns have replaced the monks.

Accommodation

Chíos Town: **Chandris Chíos**, by the sea at Prokimea, is the local businessmen's meeting place, B-class (tel: 0271-25761/8). **Kyma**, next door to Chandris, was built in Italian style with a fine painted ceiling; C-class (tel: 0271-25551/3). Mestá: **Lida**, B-class pension (tel: 0271-76217). Kambos: **Perivoli** pension, B-class is quiet (tel: 0271-31513).

Restaurants

Best fish restaurants are at Karfás, the nearest beach to

Chíos Town. **Tassos Restaurant**, 6 Livanou Street, is popular.

General Information
Population: 50,000
Area: 325sq miles (841sq km)
153 nautical miles from Piréas.
Tourist Office: 11 Kanari Street (tel: 0271-24217).
Harbour Police: tel: 0271-22837.

How to Get There
Air: Flights come from Athens at least twice daily (50mins); from Lésvos (40mins), Sámos (35mins) and Mýkonos (55mins) once or twice a week.
Ferries: From Piréas 3–7 days a week (10hrs); from Sámos (mainland) twice a week (4¾hrs); from Lésvos 3–7 days a week (4hrs); from Thessaloníki 2 days a week; from Límnos, Kavala (mainland), Ikaría, Léros, Kálymnos, Kós, Rhodes, Chálki, Kárpathos, Kásos, Crete (Siteía, Ágios Nikólaos), Santoríni, Folégandros and Mílos once a week. Ferries go daily to Oinoússes, and 3 times a week to Psará (3¾hrs). Ferries also connect with Çesme (Turkey).

LÉSVOS (LESBOS) ✓

Third largest of the Greek isles, the Greek Government calls it Lesbos, British and US tour operators usually call it Lésvos and locals and ferry companies call it Mytilíni. Relatively few visitors go, perhaps because it is not easy to explore the island without long, tiring bus journeys or without hiring a car (the only way to see much of it). And local people, though very friendly, are more interested in their 11,000 olive trees than in tourism. They provide some of the best olive oil in the world. Ferries call at the capital Mytilíni, an industrial town, but holiday-makers prefer Míthymna (Mólivos), a pretty, delightful fishing town two hours away by coach in the north. The two towns have feuded since classical times. They are only 40 miles (64km) apart, but the linking paved road is tortuous and mountainous. The easier coast road collapsed in the dreadful winter of 1986–7. The local lyric poetess Sappho was responsible for the second meaning of the word 'lesbian'. She ran a school and wrote passionate verse to her female pupils. The Orthodox church in Constantinople banned and burned most of her poems.

◆◆◆
MYTILÍNI TOWN
A busy town, it has two harbours divided by a peninsula topped by a Genoese fortress. The north harbour is commercial. The south is mostly for fishing boats and yachts. The waterfront is the heart of the town, with banks, businesses, snack bars, hotels and restaurants. Mytilíni beach is organised, with chairs, shade and a snack bar.

MUSEUMS AND SITES
Archaeological Museum: ancient sculptures and ceramics (*open*: daily, except Monday; 08.30– 15.00hrs).
Byzantine Museum: in Philanthropic Society building, has fine icons.
Old House, Mitropoleos Street: 19th-century island home, complete with working kitchen. These three museums are all in Mytilini Town.

Teriad Museum, Vareiá, 2½ miles (4km) south of Mytilíni: a superb museum, purpose-built by the Parisian art critic Teriad, in the grounds of his house, to show his private collection, which includes works by Chagall, Mirò, Picasso, Le Corbusier and many others. Also 40 paintings by the local primitive folk-artist Theophilos, which Teriad arranged to have shown in the Louvre, Paris.

Theophilos Museum, Vareiá: Theophilos (1873–1934) was an artist-tramp, painting walls in churches, tavernas and houses in return for food and ouzo. Teriad persuaded him to paint on canvas. Among 86 works here are some wonderful primitive paintings of Greek island scenes and people. The Ancient Theatre on pine-forested heights north of Mytilíni, was one of the biggest in Greece, with room for an audience of 15,000. The 13th-century Genoese fortress is well preserved, with views to the Turkish mainland.

Excursions

The road to Míthymna from Mytilíni passes the big, almost landlocked bay of Geras, then goes over mountains to Kallóni, a market town known for its fishing village, Skála Kallóni, on the huge Kólpos (Gulf) Kallonís and renowned for sardines – a rarer fish today and mostly eaten by visitors. A large sand beach has some shady trees. Just before Kallóni, 25 miles (40km) west of Mytilíni, a road into the hills leads to Agía Paraskeví, 17 miles (27km) west of Mytilíni, where they breed

Míthymna: even modern fishing nets need to be repaired

white horses. You can see lovely white mares with black foals, which turn white later. Moní Leimónos (Limonos monastery), 1523, north of Kallóni, is controlled by Mount Athos monks and bans women visitors. It has magnificent carvings and icons.

◆◆◆
MÍTHYMNA (MÓLIVOS)

Míthymna is a delightful partnership of fishing village and small tourist resort. The charming harbour, a 10-minute walk from the village, is filled with old-style wooden fishing caiques. Elegant stone houses with red roofs rise in very steep lanes and cobbled steps to the strong walls of a ruined Genoese castle, from which there are views to Turkey. In the town, cars are banished from 18.00hrs until dawn.

Tavernas along the waterfront serve a good choice of fish. Nassos, on a road leading up from the harbour, can offer lobster, sea bream, snapper, red mullet and swordfish, plus local island beef and lamb. Míthymna's long pebbly beach is a bit disappointing but buses and taxis go to the sandy beach of the quieter village Pétra, 34 miles (55km) west of Mytilíni, with the same cobbled streets and red-roofed houses, and tavernas in the main square. An unpaved road from Míthymna leads to Loutra Eftalos, 3½ miles (6km) north, a spa by the sea with very hot springs, a small beach, a taverna and two hotels, Alkeos and a Mithymna pension owned by the similarly-named hotel in Míthymna.

A paved but winding mountainous road from Kalloní leads to Ántissa, a large mountainside village, and on to Sígri, 28 miles (45km) from Kalloní, a very quiet fishing village known for its lobsters. This is walkers' country, with several good beaches and a Turkish castle in good order.

◆◆
ERESÓS

Reached by a south fork after Ántissa, 28 miles (45km) from Kalloní, the birthplace of Sappho is delightful, with a superb main square under a huge plane tree, and a lively market. The village resort Skála Eresoú, 4½ miles (7km) from Eresós, is on a wide sand beach 1½ miles (2.5km)

The beautiful setting for a monastery and its grounds near Ántissa

long and slowly expanding. It even has a disco in season. Its main square is lined with tavernas and restaurants, and there are several hotels. Fishing boats supply the tavernas. Many package tourists stay in rooms and pensions. These places in the west of the island can be reached by bus, but this is lengthy and a car is invaluable. Summer excursions from Mytilíni and Míthymna do help. In the south of the island are some beautiful routes, with lovely mountain views, but they can be rough; some not only

(25km) from Mytilíni, a village of old wooden houses with flowered balconies in steep cobbled streets on the slopes of Óros (Mount) Ólympos, in a gorgeous setting of apple orchards and woods. There is a 12th-century church with an icon said to date from AD 803 and a medieval castle.

◆◆
PLOMÁRI

Another paved road from Mytilíni rounds the gulf of Geras down the south coast to Plomári, the island's second biggest town , 43½ miles (70km) from Mytilíni. It has an old town on one side, a new one on the other, both packed close down a hillside. A busy commercial port, with an active fishing fleet, it is now also a resort, with the best beach near by at Ágios Isídoros. Plomári claims to make the best ouzo in Greece; Aphrodite, at 90 per cent proof, may be the strongest.

have boulders but sheer drops, and they wriggle and turn sharply. Take local advice. A paved road goes west from Mytilíni to Políchnitos, an elegant spa with a not very desirable beach on Kallonís Bay.
There is a better beach westward at Nyfida, 5½ miles (9km) from Políchnitos. The spa has five springs claimed to be the hottest in Europe (76°–87.6°C). A road south reaches Vatera, with a grey sand and shingle beach nearly 5 miles (8km) long, among orchards and vineyards, with pensions, rooms and tavernas. The Mytilíni–Políchnitos road passes a tortuous road on the left to lovely Agiássos, 15½ miles

Accommodation

Mytilíni: **Sappho**, on the waterfront, Prokymea Kountourioti, has character but is a bit noisy, C-class (tel: 0251-28415). **Blue Sea**, 91 Prokymea Kountourioti, convenient by the ferry quay end of harbour, is comfortable, B-class (tel: 0251-23994/5). Míthymna: **Sea Horse Hotel**, harbour quay square, is a neat and popular B-class pension (tel: 0253-71320/1). **Míthymna I**, very pleasant, near the beach, pension A-class (tel: 0253-71386). **Poseidon**, 2 Parodos Possidonos, very nice B-class pension, only 6 rooms, so book (tel: 0253-71570). B-class **Delphinia I** is 20 minutes' walk away in the hills (tel: 0253-71315). **Alkeos** has good views and swimming, but is a mile (1.5km) uphill from any tavernas, B-class (tel: 0253-71002). Eresós: **Sappho the Eressia**, 12 Theofrastou Skála, C-class (tel: 0253-53233).

Restaurants

Lésvos is very well off for locally caught fish, local beef, lamb and vegetables. **Asteria** in Mytilíni is good value. In Míthymna, **Nassos** on the road from the harbour has exceptional variety and quality. By the harbour, the **Sea Horse Hotel** restaurant and the next door taverna, **To Limani**, are good and popular. At **Georgios** (with rooms) by the beach, you eat under vines.

Genoese ramparts overlook the harbour and fishing fleet at Mýrina

General Information

Population: 88,600
Area: 629sq miles (1,630sq km)
188 nautical miles from Piréas.
Tourist Office: tel: 0251-42111.
Tourist Police: tel: 0251-22770.

How to Get There

Air: Charters via some European countries. Up to six flights daily from Athens (45mins). From Thessaloníki 6–7 weekly (1hr 20mins); from Chíos (40mins) and Sámos (55mins) 1 or 2 a week; from Rhodes 3 weekly (1hr 20mins); from Límnos 4 weekly.
Ferries: From Piréas (14hrs) 6 a week; from Chíos 6 weekly; from Thessaloníki and Kavala, Límnos and Sámos twice weekly; once a week from Léros, Kárpathos, Santoríni, Crete, Folégandros and Mílos.

LÍMNOS (LEMNOS)

Near Turkey and opposite the Dardanelles, Límnos, 185 square miles (479 sq km), population 18,000, is treeless and covered with golden pasture and grain fields. There are few beaches. The island is Greece's biggest Aegean military base. Aircraft seats from Athens are often booked weeks ahead by military families. Seats are easier to obtain on flights from Lésvos (daily, 45mins). Mainland ferries from Kavala, Rafina and Thessaloníki. Mýrina, capital and ferry port, is dominated by a Genoese castle.

THÁSOS (THASSOS)

Thásos is a softly beautiful, languid island, redolent of hot sun and the smell of pines and protected from *meltemi* winds by the mainland of Macedonia only 6¾ miles (11km) away. It is a round mountain covered with trees and little valleys where rivers run down to hidden coves or long sandy beaches, backed by olive groves, vineyards, wheat fields and vegetables. Accommodation is abundant because the island has long lured Greeks from the mainland, but relatively few foreigners get there.

◆◆

LIMENAS (THÁSOS TOWN)

Like Kós Town, Thásos has ancient remains mixed up with its modern buildings, and many are lovely, for the central peak, Ypsário, is virtually a block of marble. The main excavations:

● **The Agorá**: Entered from beside the museum, there are remains from the classical city, of passageways, shops, monuments, and an elaborate temple to Artemis. Buy a guide book, as there is little labelling.

● **The Ancient Theatre**: Set dramatically among pines overlooking a wide expanse of sea, the theatre is reached by steep steps. Performances in Greek of ancient dramas are given on Saturdays from late-July to mid-August.

● **Ancient Walls**: Exploring means a strenuous 3-mile (5km) walk past the theatre. You can follow the walls past the foundations of a 5th-century BC temple to Apollo and a small sanctuary with a relief of Pan and his goats. The 'Secret Stairs' carved into rock in the 6th century BC lead to the Gateway of Silenus, the phallic god. His massive phallus (a fertility totem) was chiselled away in the 1930s during one of those 'moral cleansing' campaigns dictators have forced on Greeks.

● **The Museum**: This contains many archaeological finds, including interesting items from the temple of Artemis.

The town has a nice fishing harbour, and typically Greek shops and tavernas.

INLAND VILLAGES AND BEACHES

The most attractive inland village is Panagía, 7½ miles (12km) from Limenas, and set among trees and springs on the slopes of the mountain, with delightful sea views. At Chrysí Aktí, a tiny resort also called Skála Potamiás, you can taste the local catch outside the tavernas. Moní Archangélou, round the coast, 23½ miles (38km) south of Thásos Town, is a convent where nuns show visitors the hollows in the stone made, they claim, by St Luke kneeling in prayer. The road continues round the coast to Potós, a small but growing resort by a big beach, with plenty of tavernas, small modern blocks of apartments and a comfortable modern hotel. A road through a lovely valley leads to the old capital, Theológos. Here you can buy Thasian honey. Pefkári, a smaller village a mile (1.5km) from Potós, has a sand beach but rocky seabed. Beyond is Limenária, an overgrown fishing village, which still has a strong German flavour as a legacy from a company which mined ore here before the 1914 war. Quiet by day, it wakes up at night to bar music and discos. Thásos has one drawback – mosquitoes. But modern devices deal with them at night. Forest fires are a hazard, too.

Accommodation

Thásos Town: **Lena**, Megalou Alexandrou, is a clean, comfortable modern hotel with balconies, all rooms with wc, shower, E-class (tel: 0593-22793). Among dozens of others, **Timoleon**, Paralia (waterfront near the ferry quay) is pleasant, B-class (tel: 0593-22177); **Aktí**, is cheaper, a clean, B-class pension (tel: 0593-22326). A recommended A-class hotel is **Roula** (tel: 0593-22905). **Makryammos Bungalow Hotel** on the private beach is A-class (tel: 0593-22101). Limenária: plenty of choice. **Hatzichristos**, vine clad and pleasant, on the beach is better than its rating; all rooms with wc, E-class (tel: 0593-51567). **Menel**, 43 Omonias is good value, C-class (tel: 0593-51396).

Restaurants

One of the best restaurants in Thásos Town is **Akrogiali** at the end of the esplanade away from the old harbour: good food.

General Information

Population: 16,000
Area: 146sq miles (379sq km)
Tourist Office & Tourist Police: Thásos Town (tel: 0593-22500).
Harbour Police: tel: 0593-71290.

How to Get There

Air: To Keramoti (mainland) then ferry (see below).
Ferries: From Kavala (mainland, 1hr 15mins) daily; from Keramoti (mainland, 35mins) 12 a day, every hour in summer, 7 a day in winter.

SPORADES

SKÍATHOS ✓

Skíathos is one of the most beautiful of the Greek islands and very popular with British families. It has gentle hills, pine and olive groves down to the sea, dense woods covering whole areas in green, long sandy beaches and wild shores, with western mountains so rugged that you can enter only on foot or mule. All this is packed into an island 8 miles (13km) long.
But it is the fine beaches which have made it popular for so long – those and the big airfield built in the 1960s. Charters brought holiday-makers from all over Europe, and with the many visitors come good restaurants and a wide choice of nightlife.

BEACHES

Dotted all round the island are sweeps of clean yellow sand. Most beaches have tavernas and restaurants, even Asélinos on the west coast, which can be reached only on foot or by caique.

Koukounariés, 7½ miles (12km) southwest of Skíathos Town, has one of the best stretches of sand in Greece – 1,094 yards (1,000m), backed by shady pines. In season a water-skiing school disturbs the calm of this tranquil spot.

A footpath from the road behind Koukounariés lagoon leads to a lovely sand beach, Mandraki, in the Bay of Xerxes.

You must take a caique from Skíathos port to Lalária in the north (1hr), where there is a dramatic beach of silver pebbles enclosed by sheer grey-white rock cliffs.

◆◆
KÁSTRO

A path across Skíathos, marked by red blobs of paint, which you can pick up at Ágios Konstandinos on the edge of Skíathos Town, takes you in 2½-3 hours to the crumbling walls of Kástro, the old Byzantine fortified town on a point with superb views. In the 16th century it had 300 houses, 22 churches and was a refuge for the island's whole population against pirates. Now all that remains is an entrance gateway, two ruined churches and a *hammam* (Turkish baths).

◆◆
SKÍATHOS TOWN

Buses are frequent on the coast road to and from Skíathos Town. Taxis cruise and the shared cost is reasonable.

Skíathos port is lively. It is divided into two by an island, now joined to the mainland by a bridge. The Venetian castle, heavily restored, is a school. The original port is used by fishing boats, the main port by ferries and cargo boats. Cars and people cram the streets in summer. The harbourside tavernas have a rather noisy happy atmosphere at night. Up

The fine beaches of Skíathos have made the island popular for a long time with discerning holiday-makers

the steps at the south end of the harbour are tiny, delightful, crowded fish tavernas.

Accommodation
Prices drop heavily off-season. Skíathos Town: **Kostis**, Evangelístrias Street, is dearer than most pensions and better (tel: 0427-42979). **Hotel Aktí** on the waterfront is good value, C-class (tel: 0427-22024). Koukounariés Beach: **Skíathos Palace**, expensive by island standards, Luxury-class (tel: 0427-22242). The **Xenia** costs about half as much, B-class (tel: 0427-22041/2).

Restaurants
There is a high standard of meals in many tavernas and restaurants, with good prawns and crab dishes. **Miramare** is the most popular on the waterfront.

General Information
Population: 4,100
Area: 18½sq miles (48sq km)
Tourist Office & Tourist Police: tel: 042-21111.
Harbour Police: tel: 0427-22017.

How to Get There
Air: Many charters fly direct from Europe. There are 3–7 flights a day from Athens (50mins).
Ferries: Daily from Vólos on the mainland (5¼hrs), where there are bus connections down to Athens; daily from Ágios Konstandinos (3¼hrs); 1–3 a week from Kými on Evia (5¼hrs); from Skópelos (½hr) and Alónnisos (2½hrs) 1 or 2 a day; 1–4 a week from Skýros.
Hydrofoils: Daily from Ágios Konstandinos, Vólos and, occasionally, Néa Moudania in Halkidiki.

SKÓPELOS

Skópelos port becomes more
sophisticated every year and
the flow of visitors has grown
mightily in recent years,
Skópelos is no longer the
dreamy, undeveloped Greek
isle of 30 years ago. It still has
very few roads with only one
bus route, and to explore it you
must use boats as buses and
walk goat tracks over hills
covered with trees – pine and
plane, silver-leafed olives,
almonds, quinces and plums,
whose fruit is made into prunes.
It is a beautiful island, especially
in spring time.

◆◆
SKÓPELOS TOWN
The town of Skópelos is beautiful,
too. Known locally as Chóra, it is
built on a steep amphitheatre
around a busy port used by
fishing boats, supply caiques and
yachts, its quay lined with café
tables. Along white-paved
streets, houses with roofs of blue
slate and red tiles rise to a
Venetian castle. Houses tend to
be taller than on most isles, and
their blue and green shutters
and balconies with flowers bring
colour to the intense whiteness.
Among them are Venetian
houses with projecting upper
storeys held by wooden beams
and internal courtyards. There
are 123 churches in the town,
some so small that you might
mistake them for cottages.
The Venetian castle was used
by the pirate Philip Gizi, who
made his base here until he was
captured. In the War of
Independence it was
headquarters for leaders of the
Greek insurrection against the
Turks. The dusty road to the
now-ruined fort is the home of
goats and donkeys. The view is
superb.
Hotels and a few discos are
mostly hidden on the far side of
the bay. The main nightly
entertainment is the *voltá* along
the quayside, then eating and
drinking in a taverna where
someone may strike up a tune on
an instrument.

◆◆
LOUTRÁKI
Loutráki has an enormous ferry
quay, looking odd beside the
little fishing village with boats
pulled up on the shingle. Except
when a ferry is due, it is a quiet,
calm place, where you can sit
outside one of the tavernas with
a cooling drink and a book and
be at peace with the world. The
ferry quay was built to service
the important agricultural centre
of Glóssa, a beautiful place in
woods up the hill. Built mostly
under the Turks, its white and
ochre houses survived the 1965
earthquake. Chickens, donkeys
and goats haunt the dusty
cobbled alleys. There is one
taverna and a small hotel, the
Avra (tel: 0424-33550).
A mule track from Makhalos, a
village south of Glóssa, takes
you to the church of Ágios
Ioannis on the rugged north
coast. It is reached by 100 steps
in the rock and is perched like
an eagle's nest over the sea.

MONASTERIES
Skópelos has 360 churches and
several monasteries. Four are
within walking distance of
Skópelos Town. Agía Varvara is
fortified; it contains frescoes

from the 15th century. Moní Evangelístria, open to visitors, has wonderful views. It has a dozen nuns – ironic, for it was founded by the monks of Mount Athos who still ban all women from their monastery. Prodromos, looking out from a craggy height to the isle of Alónissos, still has nuns in residence. Moní Metamórphosis, recently abandoned as a monastery, is used for a big August festival.

Skópelos is superb at the end of May and early June – quiet, not too hot and very green.

Accommodation
There are about 34 hotels in Skópelos Town, mostly seasonal. **Amalia** is B-class with 50 bedrooms (tel: 0424-22688); **Archontiko** is a lovely restored mansion with only 10 rooms, A-class (tel: 0424-220490).

Restaurants
Good fish is served in waterfront tavernas at Skópelos Town and Loutráki. In Glóssa, **Rania** restaurant has good views.

General Information
Population: 4,500
Area: 36½sq miles (95sq km)
Tourist Office & Tourist Police: tel: 0424-22235.
Harbour Police: tel: 0424-22180.

How to Get There
Ferries: Most people fly to Skíathos, then take the boat. Ferries from the mainland call at Skópelos Town and Loutráki (Glóssa). There are ferries daily from Vólos (4½hrs), where there are bus connections to Athens; daily from Ágios Konstandínos (4½hrs); 1–3 weekly from Kými (Evia, 3½hrs); from Alónissos 1–2 a day (½hr); from Skíathos daily (½hr); 1–4 weekly from Skýros; from Límnos 1–2 a week (7hrs).
Hydrofoils: Daily from Ágios Konstandínos and Vólos.

A dramatically sited church on Skópelos: one of the estimated 360 churches on the island

PEACE AND QUIET

Wildlife and Countryside in the Greek Islands
by Paul Sterry

With unbelievably blue seas, a wonderful climate and delightful sandy beaches, the islands are a holiday-maker's paradise. They also have a rich variety of wildlife and, despite increased tourism and development, there is much to see off the beaten track as well as in the resorts themselves. The character and climate of the islands lying to the west of the mainland in the Ionian Sea are very different from those to the east in the Aegean, the rugged Ionian Isles having almost twice as much annual rainfall as the Aegean Isles. Throughout the islands, however, most rainfall occurs during the winter months, with scarcely a cloudy day during the summer. Temperatures in the summer rise to highs of around 95°F (35°C), which has a profound effect upon the plants and animals of the region. Winter is a time for growing, and early spring the time to reproduce. Consequently, most of the flowers bloom and wither by June and many animals go into a state of summer hibernation called 'aestivation' to avoid the searing heat.

The Coasts and Seas

Because the Mediterranean is more or less land-locked, it differs from most of the world's other seas and oceans in having a minimal tidal range. This is extremely convenient for the holiday industry because it means that the beaches are always accessible. However, it

Audouin's gulls visit harbours and ports around the coasts

also means that very few inter-tidal animals and plants can live on the shoreline, although the sea has a wealth of life.
The productivity of the seas around the Greek Islands is rich indeed, as witnessed by the menus in the tavernas. The fish, squid and crustaceans are also eaten by some specialised oceanic animals. Schools of fish-eating dolphins are seen from boats, and these playful marine mammals often come close to vessels out of curiosity.

Mediterranean Monk Seal
One of the rarest sights in the region is the Mediterranean monk seal. Previously persecuted by fishermen to the point of extinction, they are now rarely seen despite their large size, their numbers having dwindled to a handful which frequent isolated coasts and islets. In the summer, the females produce their calves in inaccessible sea caves.

PEACE AND QUIET

While on boat trips you may also see flocks, known as 'rafts', of shearwaters, truly oceanic birds that fly in long lines with stiffly held wings. The brownish, Mediterranean shearwater is sometimes joined by its larger cousin, the Cory's shearwater, which resembles a miniature albatross especially when seen flying in strong winds.

On inaccessible cliffs and islets, Audouin's gulls occasionally nest. These rare and elegant seabirds resemble a small herring gull, but have a red beak and dark legs as adults. Outside the breeding season, they often wander around the coast and visit ports where the juvenile birds can be a challenge to identify.

Loggerhead turtles still try to nest on remote sandy beaches on some of the Aegean Islands. Their eggs, which lie buried in the sand, sometimes prove an irresistible temptation for beech martens, curious members of the weasel family which are

The oleander hawk moth is a large and colourful species

named after the tree rather than the habitat. Although normally creatures which prefer the cover of wooded hillsides, they can occasionally be seen on quiet beaches at dawn.

Insects

For much of the year, insect life abounds on the Greek Islands. Colourful butterflies visit the flowers of the maquis and a myriad of beetles and bugs scurry for cover. As with the flower plants, the spring is the most productive time of year to look for insects. There is plenty of vegetation for the adults to lay their eggs on and flowers to provide energy-giving nectar. Among the butterflies, the clouded yellow is a familiar sight all around the Mediterranean and particularly so in the Greek Islands, being a widespread breeding species and a famous migrant. Similarly renowned for their powers of migration are the Bath white and the Queen of Spain fritillary, the latter with beautiful metallic spangles on its underwing. The southern festoon is a speciality of Greece and its islands. Since its caterpillar's foodplant is birthwort, a plant which prefers shade, the butterflies are most commonly found around open woodlands and glades. Their amazingly colourful wings are reminiscent of a stained-glass window. Although seldom seen by day, moths are also abundant and are commonly drawn to lighted windows after dark. Most spectacular of these are the hawk moths, which sometimes feed from garden flowers at dusk. The oleander hawk moth is one of the largest and most attractive species and, as its name suggests, its caterpillars feed on the poisonous, ornamental shrub oleander and are impressive in their own right. During the height of the summer, insects are at their least numerous. However, a few species of butterfly brave the heat, but most have died off leaving their chrysalids to survive until the rains of autumn. Grasshoppers and bush-crickets are still conspicuous to the eye and to the ear, and are incredibly active in the heat.

Although not venomous, large whip snakes look menacing

Cicadas

The summer is the season for cicadas, which sing incessantly from every tree and bush on the islands. They are most impressive ventriloquists and it is almost impossible to locate them by their sound. The easiest way to see them is to look for the mud turrets which the underground larval stages make just prior to emergence. By careful observation, the emerging adults can sometimes be found early in the morning.

Reptiles and Amphibians

Being cold-blooded animals not able to maintain their body temperature, reptiles and amphibians are highly dependent upon warmth from the sun. The colder the temperature, the less active they are, and as a result, some species hibernate during the colder winter months.
With warm springs and hot summers, the islands are ideal for reptiles, and snakes and lizards abound. Because water is at a premium during the summer, frogs, toads and newts, which need standing water in which to breed, are far less frequent. However, the hardy green toad occurs on some of the Cyclades and the green tree frog croaks around the smallest of pools. The best time of year to look for snakes and lizards is in the spring. Many will have just emerged from hibernation and lie about soaking up the sun's rays. Because reptiles become more active as they get hotter, search for them early in the morning; later in the day they retreat under cover to avoid overheating. During the summer months, when the temperatures are excessive, even for a cold-blooded creature, many switch from hunting by day to a nocturnal lifestyle, and so torchlight forays can then be productive. Tortoises are the most endearing reptiles found in the

PEACE AND QUIET

Greek Islands, and are certainly the easiest to see. The most widespread species in the Ionian Islands is Hermann's tortoise. Elsewhere in the region, it has probably been introduced along with other tortoise species. In the spring, they are a familiar sight as they rustle through scrubby vegetation. Regrettably, they are often killed by cars, so if you see one trying to cross the road, help it across.

Lizards abound. Geckos are frequent visitors to villas, and scurry over almost every rock face. Green lizards are common on some of the islands – Thásos for instance – and are fond of baking in bare, open areas close to cover.

Lizards form a major part of the diet of the numerous snakes. One of the largest and most impressive of these is the large whip snake, a handsome reptile which may reach a length of 6½ feet (2m) and haunts rocky hillsides and olive groves. They are frequently seen crossing the road, so drive carefully to avoid running them over.

Scrub and Woodland

At first glance, away from the coasts most of the islands look barren and inhospitable. Typically the soil is dry and stony with small shrubs interspersed with patches of low-growing plants. Their leaves are usually leathery or waxy, to resist desiccation, and plants are often spiny to discourage grazing animals. Do not be fooled, however, by the apparent paucity and uniformity in the vegetation, because over 200 species of

flower have been found in this type of habitat. In April and May, vetches, brooms, lavenders and asphodels put on a fine display of colour, but in July, the whole landscape, with the exception of the shrubbery, evergreen plants, will have turned a uniform brown.

In some senses, this barren *phrygana* habitat – as the botanists call it – as well as the more shrubby maquis, are man-made environments, or at least man-influenced. Before colonisation, most of the islands would have been covered by evergreen woodland to an altitude of about 3,280 feet (1,000m). These woodlands have gradually been cleared over the centuries and the soils, often too poor to permit full regeneration of the forests, have developed into the typical scrubby habitats we see today. Some of the islands, such as those in the northern Aegean, still have extensive woodlands, and remnants exist on many others, where the dominant tree is the aleppo pine. The open woodland that it forms allows plenty of shrubby and herbaceous plants to grow underneath, and some of them predominate in the cleared habitats as well. Tree heather, strawberry tree, juniper and laurel contribute to the understorey, and several species of rock-roses attract butterflies to their flowers. The kermes oak, with leaves like those of a miniature holly, is typical of the scrubby *phrygana* habitat, but also occurs in the shade of maquis and any remnants of aleppo pine woodland. Like the olive trees with which it often grows, it provides cover for nesting birds such as the Ruppell's warbler. This delightful songster has a pronounced, white 'moustache', which separates its black hood and throat. Although common on almost all the islands, it is not at all widespread on the mainland.

Agricultural Land

Most Greek islands are fringed by coastal alluvial plains, and the fertile, loamy soil is perfect for cultivation. Even comparatively barren and stony soils are now coming under the plough, being used to grow vines and other hardy plants. Apart from the crops themselves, these cultivated areas support a variety of birds and insects, and are particularly rewarding if they are irrigated.

Surprisingly few of the crop-producing shrubs, trees and woody plants of the islands are actually native to the region. Figs, pomegranates and olives all probably came from the Middle East, and even the grape-vine probably came from Asia. Some plants have even more exotic origins, with oranges and peaches coming from China and peppers and tomatoes from the New World. However, all these plants needed very little encouragement and now thrive throughout the Mediterranean. Like many of the native species, the cultivated plants generally grow during the mild, wet winter months. This gives them a head-start before the onset of the hot, dry summer. Many of the blossom trees, such as almond and apricot, flower from December to January, and oranges bear ripe fruit from the start of the new year.

Cultivated fields can be excellent areas for the birdwatcher on the Greek Islands. Almond trees and fruit groves provide shade from the sun and nesting sites for birds such as serins. Shrikes are common visitors to orchards

Black-eared wheatears are boldly marked and alert birds

PEACE AND QUIET

and drop to the ground the instant they see a rustling insect or lizard. Several species pass through the islands on migration, and red-backed shrikes occasionally nest. They have the rather gruesome nickname 'butcher birds', after their habit of impaling their prey on thorns or barbed wire.

Fields around the coast can be thronged with small birds during the spring migration and several species stay to nest. Black-eared wheatears, resplendent in their black, fawn and white plumage, hop from rock to rock in search of insects. Short-toed larks, on the other hand, creep around slowly, looking more like mice than birds. They seem to have a natural ability to keep to the furrows and scraps of vegetation and can be very difficult to spot. For all their apparent secrecy, they are not especially shy, and will sometimes walk right up to a quiet and stationary observer.

Hills and Mountains

Although best known for their coasts, many Greek islands have hills and mountains rising above 3,280 feet (1,000m). Among the highest at 5,315 feet (1,620m), is Mount Aïnos on Kefalloniá, lying within the boundaries of a national park. Like most other mountains in the Ionian Isles, it is composed of limestone, which encourages an interesting flora to develop. The hillsides have often been cleared of woodland and are heavily grazed by goats. This exposes flowering plants to the baking sun throughout the year,

Greek silver firs still cloak mountain tops in Kefalloniá

and because the soils are often dry and porous, only hardy species like squills, irises, crocuses and star-of-Bethlehem can survive; these flower from March to May. Pride of place, however, goes to the orchids which abound on the hills, and the varieties of tongue and bee orchids are a major attraction for botanists in spring. Mountain-tops above 3,280 feet (1,000m) are sometimes still covered by coniferous woodland. In Ionian islands like Kefalloniá, the dominant tree is the Greek silver fir, a speciality of the region. Only shade-tolerant plants can grow under its dense canopy, but hellebores, cyclamens and squills might all be found. During the summer, rocky hillsides on almost all the Greek Islands are the haunt of Cretzschmar's buntings. With their brick-red plumage and blue head, these attractive little birds are another speciality of the region. In the skies above, griffon and Egyptian vultures may soar overhead, on the look-out for carrion, and they are often joined by that most spectacular of fliers, the alpine swift. With its striking, pied plumage, this master of the air is half as big again as the common swift.

Bird Migration

Most of the islands have far fewer breeding bird species than adjacent areas on the mainland. This is due in part to the rugged nature of the landscape and uniformity of the terrain. Freshwater marshes and extensive areas of natural woodland are unusual and so the resident birds tend to be species which prefer open country. Visit during spring or autumn migration, however, and the numbers and varieties of species to be found increase dramatically. Many birds from northern Europe spend the winter south of the Mediterranean, and pass through Greece on their way back north in the spring.

In April and May, when the winds are from a favourable southerly direction, thousands of small birds will pass through the islands. If conditions remain good for migration, most will stay only briefly, but if the wind direction changes or a front passes over, they may stay and feed for a longer period. Common and black-eared wheatears, black redstarts and tawny pipits frequent sandy fields where they search the furrows for insects. They are commonly joined by flocks of turtle doves who peck at seedheads and flowers, while in the skies above, colourful and noisy flocks of bee-eaters glide their way northwards.

Autumn migration is less pronounced than in spring, but goes on for longer, so from July until October, adult birds and their offspring drift down through the islands. During July and August, brilliant blue rollers are a conspicuous feature as they perch on wires and bushes, ever alert for passing insects. Young birds of all species are generally less skilled at navigation, so you are more likely to find unusual species at this time of the year.

Eleanora's Falcon

The islands play host to a most unusual bird of prey. During the summer, the cliffs are the haunt of Eleanora's falcons, whose mastery of the air enables them to catch other birds on the wing. Unlike most other European birds, they nest in the autumn, which may at first seem rather peculiar. However, they take advantage of the vast numbers of migrant songbirds passing through Greece in the autumn, and consequently their young seldom go short of food.

Turtles

Long before European tourists discovered the sandy beaches of Greece, they were visited by loggerhead turtles. For these superbly adapted marine reptiles, their visits to dry land are not recreational, but are a matter of necessity for the survival of the species.

PEACE AND QUIET

For most of the year, loggerheads are found in the deeper Mediterranean waters, where they feed mainly on jellyfish. During spring and early summer, however, they move into shallower water and are often seen from small boats. When they judge the time is right, the females come ashore to lay their eggs in the sand. Although superbly adapted to the marine environment, with powerful flippers and a streamlined shell, they are lumbering and vulnerable on land and to avoid predators they come ashore only at night. After dragging herself up the beach, the female turtle digs a deep hole in the sand in which she lays her eggs. When the clutch is completed, it is covered over with sand and the eggs are left to their fate. Although the whole process may take several hours, egg-laying is almost always finished before dawn and the only

Loggerhead turtles hatching on a secluded sandy beach

indication that the beach has been visited will be tell-tale tracks in the sand to and from the sea. The speed at which the eggs develop depends upon the temperature of the sand, but generally takes a couple of months. Then during September or October a remarkable thing happens. Early one morning the sand will erupt as all the hatchlings from a nest burst out of the ground and rush to the sea. Unfortunately, many do not even make it to the water, falling prey to various predators, and of those that do, only one or two survive to adulthood.

Turtles are easily discouraged from egg-laying by lights or noise, so it is not surprising that they have deserted many of their ancestral beaches. Nests are also frequently raided by dogs or pigs, or even by man, and so now the turtles only visit a few remote beaches. Fortunately, the Greek authorities are aware of the conflict of interests between turtles and tourists and some beaches on islands like Kefalloniá and Zákynthos are protected for the turtles' benefit. As the species is on the brink of extinction, it is imperative that the nesting sites are not disturbed. Tourists should stay well away from the nesting beaches and refrain from powered watersports.

Spring Flowers

Mediterranean summers may suit holiday-makers, but they present real difficulties for the flowering plants of the region. The hot, dry climate causes problems with desiccation, and much of the woodland which

Flowers like the yellow bee orchid abound in spring

would have provided shade has been cleared. To add to this, the soils are porous, so any rain that does fall soon soaks away. Not surprisingly, the plants that are most successful are those with underground storage systems such as rhizomes or bulbs. During the comparatively mild and wet winters, they produce leaves, grow and store food underground and eventually flower in the spring. For a brief period, from March to May, the landscape looks green and colourful, but thereafter the leaves wither away and by July, all the vegetation, with the exception of the evergreen shrubs, has turned a uniform brown. The food stored in the bulbs and rhizomes is enough to see the plants through to the autumn. The best areas for spring flowers are the open *phrygana* and maquis type habitats. Rock-roses, with their waxy leaves and crinkly flowers, provide shelter for low-growing squills, crocuses, iris and daffodils and many of the flowers, such as the grape hyacinths, will be familiar as cultivated forms to gardeners. Orchids are common on almost all the islands and it is not unusual to notch up a dozen species or more in a single week. Spectacular species like the bug orchid, with its strong-smelling flowers, and the naked man orchid are widespread, but for sheer variety, the bee orchid family is a clear winner. Although all the bee orchids conform to a basic pattern – with a large, rounded lower flower-lip – the diverse shapes, colours and forms are astonishing. Some, like the yellow bee orchid, are widespread in the Mediterranean region while others, such as the Greek spider orchid, are restricted to Greece and its islands.

The onset of autumn in the Mediterranean is not accompanied by the die-back in vegetation so familiar in northern Europe. Instead, the milder, wetter climate following the oppressive summer induces a form of second spring. It becomes green again and new sets of flowers begin to bloom.

Seasonal Wildlife Highlights Throughout the Greek Islands

● **March** – first flush of spring flowers and insects appears in the fields and open country.

● **April** – best month for flowers and especially orchids. Migrant birds start passing through the region. Bird song can be heard in scrub and olive groves.

● **May** – late bird migrants such as bee-eaters appear. Late-flowering plants are in bloom, earlier species having begun to die back and turn brown.

● **June** – most annual flowers have withered and turned brown. Snails begin to cluster on dry stems - 'aestivating' or resting through the dry summer. Colourful butterflies abound. Turtles nest on remote beaches.

● **July** – a quiet month for land birds and flowers. Seabirds can be seen on many of the ferry crossings. Such as between mainland Greece (Kylini) and Kefalloniá and Zákynthos, or

Náxos to Páros and Mýkonos to Ermoúpoli (on Sýros) or Tínos.

● **August** – Eleanora's falcons feed on returning migrant birds around the coasts and cliffs of the Greek Islands. Rollers – bright blue birds – are a familiar sight on many islands.

● **September** – migrant bird numbers are at their highest. Bad weather induces birds to become grounded. A flush of autumn-flowering plants appear.

Bird Trapping

Early autumn, tens of millions of songbirds fly south from northern Europe to Africa for the winter. As they pass through the Mediterranean countries, millions of them never make it any further, falling victim to the 'sportsmen' of the region. Similar tactics are also employed towards the songbirds which, like the song thrush, spend the winter in the mild climate of Greece and its islands.The methods employed by the hunters are varied. Guns are used against birds of prey and herons, while nets, traps and snares are used for small birds. Perhaps most insidious of all is the technique of liming twigs and branches, where a sticky glue holds the victim's feet until it either dies of starvation or is collected by the hunter.

Some of the birds which die in Greece are killed for no better reason than to be served as delicacies, while others are sacrificed in the name of 'sport'. Fortunately, this pursuit is widely publicised outside Greece, and in response to public opinion the authorities will, hopefully, implement restrictive legislation.

SHOPPING AND SOUVENIRS

Most smaller islands have 'supermarkets', which are really little serve-yourself grocer's shops. They sell drinks, including ouzo and wine. Bakers normally sell pies, especially cheese ones, and simple cakes. Seasonal tourist shops sell postcards, 'Greek' clothes made for tourists (similar on every island, but often attractive), and sometimes such specialist clothes as hand-knitted sweaters. Simple wool sweaters can be cheap even by British standards, and some are oiled for fishermen. But they are not fashionable or sophisticated

A typical souvenir of a Greek island holiday is a string of 'worry beads'

in any way. Jewellery on these islands is imported from Athens and Mýkonos. Mýkonos sells gold jewellery at inflated prices. You can see a few last potters at work on Sífnos.

Apart from clothes, wine and liquor, the tourist shops offer pottery and ceramics, hand-woven carpets and cloth, long-haired rugs (*flokati*), hand-embroidered clothes (usually in old-fashioned styles), lace, carved or turned wooden ornaments, 'Greek' shoulder bags, sponges (Kálymnos is the 'sponge isle'), reproduction icons, jewellery in ceramics, gold or silver, marble or onyx carvings, and worry beads (*komboloi*). Many sell honey and pistachio nuts. With little outstanding to buy as souvenirs, it is all a matter of cost and taste.

FOOD AND DRINK

Greek food may not always be the best in the world, but the views from taverna tables can make up for it

FOOD AND DRINK

(Please refer to the **What to See** *section for restaurants and island specialities)*

Eating is very much a happy social occasion, rather than a serious gourmet experience, and no-one goes to Greece for the food or wine. Dishes are mostly Turkish in origin, as in all the Balkans occupied for long by the Turks, but never mention this to the Greeks. Nor does Turkish Delight exist. It is 'Greek Delight'. Surprisingly few spices are used in Greek food, but they use quite a lot of herbs, especially oregano. You

notice little salt and pepper, so popular dishes can seem a little tasteless, like meatballs (*kefthedes*) and cheese pie (*tiropita*, often bought hot from the baker's for a meal or snack). Other popular pastry pies include chicken (*kotopita*), spinach (*spanakopita*), courgette (*kolokithopita*) and the expensive favourite, lamb (*arnáki*).

Fish

It is advisable to like fish when visiting the Greek Islands. It is nearly always good, often superb, bought as it is landed and sometimes in the pan within two or three hours. Prices have gone up for three reasons – over-fishing, more tourists to feed and high prices paid by Athens restaurants tempting islanders to export. Sometimes fish is fried or, if very large, baked. But generally it is grilled – and, alas, sometimes over-grilled in tavernas where the family try to do too many things at once. However, if you are proudly shown some fresh fish, you should order it: the cook will take good care of it. Red mullet (*barboúnia*) and sea bream (*sinagrítha*) are good and pricey. *Maríthes* (whitebait), baby squid (*kalamarákia*) and octopus (*oktapóthi*) are cheaper. Lobster (*astakós*) is expensive but cheaper than in many countries.

Meat

Since Greece joined the European Union, pork has been gradually ousting lamb as the most-common meat. It is imported and much cheaper, and used extensively now instead of lamb for *souvlakia* (kebab: meat, tomato and onions grilled on a skewer). Meat is grilled or casseroled with vegetables. Apart from tomato, few sauces are served. A squeeze of lemon replaces them. Dishes are often tastier in islands once occupied by the Italians – and better cooked. Moussaka, favourite dish of most visitors, was really a feast and birthday treat on the Islands, when it was made with lamb and plenty of aubergines. To satisfy tourist demands, they often use beef and potato these days.

Salads and Starters

Greek salads and starters are delicious. *Tzatsiki* (dip of yoghurt, garlic, grated cucumber and olive oil) is best when made with local farm yoghurt (it should be sheep's milk), but even on small isles some tavernas now use large tins of it imported from Athens. *Taramosalata*, the paste of smoked fish roe, is delicious with bread and wine before the main course. Tomato and cucumber salad (*angouri domata*) is improved by a little red and green peppers. Vegetables (usually tomatoes, courgettes or aubergines) stuffed with mince or rice (*yemitses*) are served hot or cold as starters, vegetables or main dish. Vine leaves stuffed with mince or rice (*dolmades*) can be served the same way, or very small ones are served as snacks with drinks.

The great tourist standby is called Greek salad by visitors, village salad by most tavernas, and *horiatiki* by Greeks. Usually it is made of tomato and cucumber wedges, sliced onion and red and green peppers in olive oil, with olives, oregano, salt and pepper, topped with slices of feta (goat cheese) sprinkled with oregano. Cheeses can be goat, sheep or (more rarely) cow. A blue cheese is called *rockfor* (Roquefort!) and a Gruyère-style *graviera*. Goat cheese dusted with flour and fried in olive oil or grilled (*saganaki*) can be very good. *Kasseri* is said to be like Cheddar but it is usually made from sheep's milk.

Fruit and Puddings

Fruit is delicious (melon, grapes, apricots, apples, wild or cultivated strawberries, according to season and island). Greek yoghurt is excellent. Though formal restaurants may serve desserts, few island

FOOD AND DRINK

tavernas do (except ice-cream).
You might get crême caramel,
yoghurt with honey and walnuts,
honeycakes (*baklavá*), honey
puffs (*loukoumádes*), or
semolina cake with almonds,
cinnamon and lemon (*halvá*).
There are a few formal
restaurants with white table-
cloths on smaller islands.
Tavernas are the best places to
eat Greek food. Of these, the
best ask you into the kitchen to
see the fish and meat on the
slab waiting to be cooked and
other dishes bubbling in copper
pans on the stove.
If you order all your meal at
once, it will arrive all together
on cold plates. Try salads with
some wine first, then go to pick
your main dish.
Menus as presented are just a
rough guide. Restaurants and

tavernas buy what is good and
cheap at the market.

Drink

Cafés (*kafeneíons*) serve 'Greek'
coffee, which is Turkish coffee
to us, with mud in the bottom:
sweet is *glyko*, medium is *metrio*,
sugarless is *sketo*. Nescafé is
sometimes called 'American'
coffee, and served iced without
milk or sugar, it is *frappé*.
Ouzo (Greek pastis) is cruder
than French but served the
same way (iced with water).
Retsina (resinated white wine)
originated 3,000 years ago when
Greece was exporting oil and
wine in jars sealed with plaster
and resin. They believed that
resin preserved wine, which it
does not. Either you think it tastes
like camphor balls or paraffin
and hate it, or think it an ideal
accompaniment to Greek food.
The isle of Kefalloniá makes the
best dry white wine (Robola) and
also a muscat sweet wine rivalling
the renowned muscat of Sámos.
There are reliable brand wines
which you can buy on all except
the smallest isles, such as
Demestica (red and white),
Santa Helena (one of the better
dry whites), and Achaia Clauss
wines. Dry white Hymettus from
near Athens is often available.
Otherwise most islands drink
their own wine and import a
little from an island near by.
White and red wines are
produced on Kós, Thásos,
Ándros, Náxos, Íos, and Mílos.
Reds in particular come from
Corfu (try Ropa), Lefkáda (very
dark wine called Santa Mavra),
Limnos (Mavro Kalpaki),
Euboea (Halkidas), Páros (good
deep red, made from Mandilari

*The fruit you get on the Greek Isles
is delicious: make the most of it*

grape), Ikaría, Santoríni (very
strong wines around 17 per cent:
Santoríni and Vinsanto, much
sought by Greeks themselves,
and especially sweet Thira),
and a big producer of powerful
red wines, Crete (Malvazia,
Mavro Romeika, Peza, Daphnes,
Creta). Mavrodaphne, strong
sweet red wine, is drunk
everywhere. Zákynthos (Zante)
has a refreshing dry, white
'green' (young) wine called
Verdea. Greek beer is made
now by French, Danish and
Dutch brewers, is mostly lager,
and is expensive compared to
wine. For brandy, most Greeks
use the name of the big
producer Metaxa (3, 5 and 7
star). It is a bit rough for drinking
on its own, but is useful for
mixed drinks such as brandy
sour and Alexander.
Drinkable fruit-flavoured spirits
are made, some dry as aperitifs,
some sweet as liqueurs.

ACCOMMODATION

Accommodation has improved
greatly on the Greek Isles but
on very small islands there are
few hotels or pensions.
In private houses and cheaper
pensions showers can be
eccentric. Often they have fixed
heads forced round to point at
the loo and the towel rail, so do
not take towels or clothing into
the room. A slow central drain in
the floor ensures an ankle-deep
flood. Water is precious on
some small isles. It may go off
for part of the day.
Only a few island hotels are
specifically recommended in
this book (see under individual
island), simply because nearly

Hotel Gradings
De luxe, A, B, C, D and E. In
hotels down to 'B' grade all
rooms have private bathrooms;
in grade 'C' some have private
bathrooms; in grade 'D' and 'E'
private facilities seldom exist.

all hotels are fairly small and are
liable to be fully booked. Avoid
booking half-board where
possible. Eating out at tavernas
or café-bars is part of the scene
and the best way to meet people.
If you want Holiday Inn comfort,
stay in Rhodes, Corfu, Crete,
Athens or a mainland resort.
There are, however, a few big,
fairly luxurious hotels on large
isles such as Kós and Mýkonos.

**If You Arrive Without
Somewhere to Stay:**
● You will see notices such as
'room rent' on private houses.
In mid-summer, especially
when the ferry arrives late in
the day, do not be too choosy
on the first night. At other times
see the room first.
● If you cannot find a room, ask
in a taverna after buying a drink.
● Locals often meet ferries,
offering rooms. These can be a
long walk away and will almost
certainly entail sharing the
house WC and shower.
● Pay a little extra, if possible,
for a pension or small hotel.
These are likely to be very
good value on bigger isles
such as Kós, Páros, Zákynthos
and Skiathos. On small islands
they are more likely to be basic
but you may have your own
toilet and shower and they are
very cheap.

WEATHER AND WHEN TO GO

Mid-summer (late June, July, August) can be very hot, though the *meltemi* (cool northern wind) provides welcome relief from the heat. The Saronic Isles have their own wind – the north-easterly *greggo*. Take a hat and beach-cover clothes. In other months you will need a sweater

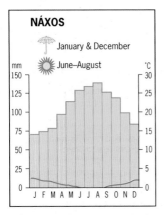

NÁXOS

January & December

June–August

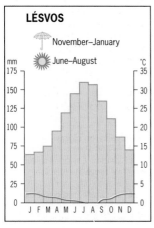

LÉSVOS

November–January

June–August

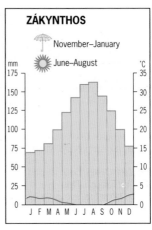

ZÁKYNTHOS

November–January

June–August

and trousers for evenings. If visiting monasteries, you need a reasonably long skirt, long trousers for men, and something long-sleeved. There is little use for formal clothes on small isles. If hopping around islands, you must necessarily be something of a backpacker. Do not take more than you can carry comfortably. But do include spare shoes (one sturdy pair), a light sweater and a complete change of clothes. Do not gamble on washing and drying clothes over night – the water may go off. Greek islands are not normally prepared for winter visitors (central heating is very rare). The tourist season is basically April to October.

NIGHTLIFE

Only on big islands or in international hotels is there formal nightlife. But discos of a sort open in cellars, old barns, windmills or bars during the tourist season. You will find one

Like these locals, you may have to wait a long time at a taverna table

on all but the tiniest isles. Bars specialise either in pop music or Greek music. Most Greeks – especially men – will dance on any excuse. Inpromptu taverna and bar dance evenings are the most fun. Live bouzouki music is played in some tavernas. Bouzoukias are night clubs where the music is professional entertainment rather than just Greek exuberance.
Most visitors prefer to have a long meal with wine in or outside a taverna, and see if music and dancing follow.

HOW TO BE A LOCAL

● Never try to hurry a Greek – it is very bad manners. Never appear even to be in a hurry.
● 'Fast food' restaurants are common on all tourist islands, but service in tavernas can be slow. Be prepared to sit a long time at a taverna table and just enjoy the scene. Eating is a

social occasion, and a meal is expected to last all evening.
● To speak quietly, to be friendly, are signs of good manners. Greeks are polite and helpful and will respond immediately if you are the same. They also love to talk, so if you learn just a few words of Greek you will be an instant success. Never snap your fingers or shout at a waiter or waitress. Never approach a Greek girl without an introduction.
● The siesta is still observed almost everywhere in summer. Noise, including driving scooters and motorcycles is forbidden between 14.00hrs and 17.00hrs; offices and shops are closed, cafés and tavernas open – in theory, but you may have to wake the owner from his nap.
● Bargaining is simply not done in hotels, restaurants, big shops, kiosks. It *is* done at street stalls or markets (except for food), so do not be shy. You may be able to negotiate a discount in smaller pensions if you stay more than three nights.

CHILDREN

The Greeks love children, and like to keep them with them until late in the evening. So you will find no problem in taking children out to eat with you. There is little entertainment especially for children in the islands, but good beaches are the main thing families look for on holiday, and most Greek beaches are safe and ideal for children. The sea is perfect for little ones to swim in.

If your children are not used to the hot sun, do make sure that you take high factor protection cream. Hats are advisable: the mid-summer sun is extremely fierce in Greece.

You may be able to find rooms in private houses, like these picturesque ones on the harbour in Milos

TIGHT BUDGET

Getting around the Greek Isles on a tight budget is not quite so easy since the clamp-down on sleeping on beaches, but is easier than almost any other country.

● You can walk into a taverna and order simply a salad.

● Rooms in people's houses are very cheap; the facilities may be basic, but will usually be clean.

● Ferry fares are fixed by the Greek Government, but you can often get cheap tourist or even deck class on big ferries from Piréas (Athens). However, tourist areas can be awash with luggage and uncomfortable in summer heat on long runs. Toilets can be awful.

● If hitch-hiking, look clean.

DIRECTORY

Contents

Arriving

(*See also individual islands.*)

● **By Air**: There are scheduled flights to Athens from all over the world and to Kós from many European countries. There are connecting flights from Athens to Atkion (for Lefkáda), Kefalloniá, Chíos, Kós, Límnos, Léros, Lésvos (Mytilíni), Mílos, Mýkonos, Páros, Sámos, Santoríni, Skíathos, Skýros, Zákynthos. Athens airport is divided into two: West (Olympic Airlines domestic and international flights) and East (other international airlines). Allow time for connecting flights. Charter flights (cheaper) are legion from Europe to many islands in high summer, but from the US nearly all charters go to Athens, Rhodes or Crete. Under Greek law, you must be given an accommodation voucher with these cheap flights. Often it is for a campsite or a room in a private house. You do not have to use it, but it must be for actual accommodation.

● **By Ferry**: Ferries go to most

islands from Piréas, the port of Athens, although they go also to a few islands from Rafina and Lavrion (both reached by bus from Athens), and Ágios Konstandinos, Kavala, Keramoti, Kými, Kyllini, Patras, Thessaloníki and Vólos (all on the mainland). There are also fast hydrofoil services to some islands from Piréas, Lavrion, Ágios Konstandinos, Kými, Thessaloníki and Vólos. (For routes, see under individual islands.) There are three basic ways of seeing the islands. You can take a package to a fairly big island and explore it thoroughly, taking an excursion or two to a smaller isle. Or you can pick bed and breakfast, or just a bed, on an isle which has ferries to three or four others, use this as a base to leave most of your luggage, and stay overnight in rooms at any of the other isles if you want or if you cannot get a ferry back. Or you can island hop. This needs as much time as possible, and patience. Ferries to and from some smaller isles are not frequent and can be cancelled because of ill winds at some times of year. Because of ferry times, you can often see twice as many isles in three weeks as in a fortnight.

Do check ferry sailings and times right up to the day you are going: ferries can be out of action and even switched to another island if it is festival time there! The port police are helpful and give friendly advice on ferry times, but often only speak Greek so you need pencil and paper. For most ferries you must buy your ticket from a local agent – often the grocer's shop – but do not rely on the agent for information. Agents look after rival companies and will not tell you that another boat exists (especially true in Piréas). Asking in a taverna can be more reliable. Tickets can sometimes be purchased on the quayside or aboard the ferries.

More ferries run from about mid-May to early September, and in June, July and August there may be many excursions to other islands. One trick is to take an excursion and jump ship, but do tell the boat crew. Above all, leave time to get the aircraft home. If you miss a charter flight, you cannot transfer to another, and a scheduled flight will cost you dear.

● **Visas**: No visas are needed by Britons, other EU members, US citizens, Canadians, Australians or New Zealanders for stays up to three months. No foreigner is supposed to work in Greece without a work permit. Penalties for illegal working are severe.

Baby Equipment

Do not count on small island pharmacies or grocers stocking your particular brand of baby-milk or food. It is safest to bring your own. Disposable nappies (diapers) are available, except on very small isles.

Camping

Camping outside official sites has been illegal since 1977. Officially this was because hordes of young people camped on or alongside beaches and caused sanitation and fire hazards. An unstated reason was an official policy to upgrade tourism and to discourage hippies or young people with no money to spend. The authorities believed that youngsters without money would turn to crime in order to eat, and their hanging around beaches, bars and cafés discouraged other visitors. 'Private' campsites are usually cheap, unofficial, and have minimal facilities. Official sites, with fairly good facilities, are dearer. Obtaining gas cylinders for cookers can be difficult in some areas. *Never* light an open fire: you will probably get two to three months in prison.

Until recently, it was possible, though illegal, to sleep on beaches in a sleeping bag. The police have clamped down on this and you could easily end up in jail, not a good idea in Greece.

Crime

Greek islanders are mainly extremely honest. Virtually all robberies and petty thefts from pockets, rooms or cars are done by foreign visitors who run out of money. See **Police**, page 121. **Drugs**: In no circumstances take illegal drugs into Greece – you will do a long stretch in a primitive prison. If you take medical drugs, take a doctor's certificate with them.

Domestic Travel

Hiring self-drive transport can be a problem on isles with rough roads. Only hire a motorcycle if you are an accomplished and steady rider. Mopeds can be very dangerous and some package-tour operators actively discourage moped hire. Servicing is slack, so make absolutely sure that brakes and steering are good. Italian mopeds are giving way to automatic Japanese models. Up steep hills, or up fairly reasonable hills with two aboard, they may stop or jump out of gear.

It is vital to have good medical insurance for Greece. Before hiring a vehicle, make certain that you are covered for road accidents. Many policies are void for mopeds.

● **Car Rental** As Greece is in the EU, valid British driving licences are accepted. Americans will probably need an International Driving Licence. Car rental is expensive, with tax and mileage added, but it is the best way of seeing most islands, especially real old farming villages. Rewards are great. You need care and some courage to drive dirt mule tracks which pass for roads. You *must* have a collision waiver, otherwise you can be charged outrageously for a scratch and pay up to £500 of repair bills whether the damage was your fault or not. Be careful of cut-price local hire firms. Their servicing is often

Hydriot children in national costume on one of the island's festival days

appalling, they may refuse the accident waiver clause and take little interest if you break down. Check brakes, tyres, including spare, before renting. If possible, rent from Avis, Eurocar or Hertz, even if it costs more. Fill up with petrol when you can – garages are scarce in country districts.

● **Speed Limits** Private vehicles: Built-up areas 31mph (50kph); outside built-up areas 43mph (70kph); motorways 62mph (100kph). You must carry fire extinguishers; first aid kit, breakdown warning triangle. Undipped headlights must not be used in towns.

● **Maps** Some local island maps are a joke. Uncompleted or planned-but-not-started roads may be marked. Hard-earth mule tracks are marked as roads because local people use them. Do not shy away from them or you will miss a lot, but watch for transmission-shattering

DIRECTORY

Idyllic peace and quiet on the waterfront, Zákynthos

projecting boulders. Michelin map 980 of Greece is very useful but does not show these minor roads which you will need to explore properly. Do not worry if you get lost. There are not enough roads for you to be lost for long.

• **Car Breakdown** Motoring organisations are not well represented on most Greek isles, but there are competent mechanics and vehicle repair shops in most villages.

• **Buses** These vary greatly from isle to isle in frequency and routes. Timetables are usually posted outside tavernas or cafés by main stops, but are somewhat unreliable. Buses can be early or very late. Mid-summer they are very crowded and you may have to stand on one foot and fight to get on or off at intermediate stops. There is no orderly queuing to get on but you will not be left behind if it is humanly possible to squeeze you on – all part of Greek-island life.

• **Taxis** In high summer it pays to share taxis, which cost more than buses but have great advantages. To tour an island in a day, find three or four people to share a taxi with you, agree the cost before you set out and try to pick an English-speaking driver who can tell you about the passing scene.

Electricity

Generally 220 volts, though 110 on some remote isles. Two-pronged plugs are common – take a plug adaptor for shavers, irons, hairdryers, etc.

Embassies and Consulates

Great Britain: 1 Ploutarchou Street, Athens 106 75 (tel: 01-723 6211-19). 24 Akti Possidonis, Piréas (tel: 01-417 8345).

USA: 91 Vasilissis Sofias Avenue, Athens 115 21 (tel: 01-721 2951/9).

Canada: 4 Ioannou Gennadiou Street, Athens 115 21 (tel: 01-723 9511/9).

Australia: 37 D Soutsou Street, Athens 115 21 (tel: 01-644 7303).

New Zealand: 15-17 An. Tsochou Street, Athens 115 21 (tel: 01-641 0311/5).

Emergency Numbers
See **Police** for each island.

Entertainment Information
On posters or ask in tavernas.

Hazards
Mosquitoes are a curse in Greece. Take the usual precaution of not opening a window with the light on. But do take an electric mosquito killer with an adaptor plug. They are a superb invention. Coils smell. Some lotions are effective, too: try Jaico Anti-mosquito Milk.

Health
Under EU agreements, European visitors can receive free medical treatment. You must have a current E111 form before leaving home. But do take out extra medical insurance. For serious illness it is essential. Some package tours offer medical insurance at extra charge. Make sure that the policy covers motor accidents and the cost of an air taxi (needed on some isles to take you to a bigger island, or to Athens). Better still, have a policy which will fly you home in an emergency. The European health Advocacy also provides a range of services in a number of languages. Contact Kolofontas 3, Athens (tel: 01-723 4621). Many Greek hospitals are poorly equipped and staffed. Private doctors are expensive. You will have to pay and claim on your insurance when you return. There should be at least one doctor (*iatrós*) on each island (hours usually 09.00– 13.00hrs; 17.00–19.00hrs). Hospitals occur less frequently. Outpatients clinics are held in the mornings.

The Tourist Police on each island will be able to supply addresses and phone numbers.

Health Regulations
No special immunisation needed, but check that your shots are up to date – typhoid-cholera, tetanus, polio.

Holidays
Each island has a holiday on its Saint's Day and on annual festival days. For the following national holidays *all* shops and businesses shut (except perhaps the baker's shop), and also close on the afternoon before.
Orthodox Easter is a great two-day festival of religious services and processions. The date varies.
1 January – New Year's Day.
6 January – Epiphany.
25 March – Greek Independence Day.
Shrove Monday.
Good Friday.
Easter Sunday.
Easter Monday.
1 May – May Day (Labour Day).
7 June – Day of the Holy Spirit.
15 August – Assumption of the Virgin Mary.
28 October – Ochi Day (anniversary of Metaxas saying *Ochi* (No) to Mussolini's demands in World War II).
25 December – Christmas.
26 December – Boxing Day.

Lost Property
Go to the police if only for insurance purposes, but unless the property is very valuable, they take little interest.

Money Matters
Credit cards are not used on the islands except in higher grade hotels and restaurants and more expensive shops in the bigger

DIRECTORY

towns. Travellers' cheques are sometimes suspect outside these establishments or banks (*trápeza*). Normal banking hours are 08.00hrs to 13.30 or 14.00hrs (usually closed Saturdays and Sundays). The main banks are the National Bank of Greece and the Commercial Bank of Greece. Most small islands have no bank. Usually there is an exchange office in a travel agent or grocer's shop, but watch exchange rates here, and in big hotels. Foreign currency is always in demand, especially dollars, pounds sterling and deutschmarks. British bank cheques are cashed in banks displaying the EC (Eurocheque) sign, but you must present a Eurocheque card. Home bank cards are not accepted outside Britain or the US. You may take 100,000 drachmas into Greece in local currency, but may export only 20,000 in denominations of 1,000.

Nudism

Nudism is still banned on all but a very few nudist beaches. There are, on some islands, remote beaches where nudism is tolerated; for example, at Krássa, now called Banana Beach because you can peel off everything, on Skíathos. Topless sunbathing has become more general, and is tolerated except in the centre of town. On Kós, for instance, it is usual alongside the harbour bay in Kós Town.

Opening Times

Banks: Monday to Friday 08.00–13.30 or 14.00hrs, some open Saturdays in big towns.
Museums: closed on Mondays or Tuesdays; normally other weekdays 08.30–15.00hrs, outdoor sites to 19.00hrs. Winter hours are usually shorter.
Post Offices: Monday to Friday 07.00–15.00hrs.
Shops: open in summer Tuesday, Thursday and Friday 08.30–13.30 and 17.30–20.30hrs; Monday, Wednesday and Saturday 08.30–14.00hrs. But in tourist areas in summer they usually open Monday to Saturday 08.00–13.00hrs, then 17.00 until 20.30–22.00hrs. Souvenir and tourist shops open on Sundays.

Pharmacies

For minor complaints, Greeks consult pharmacists (*farmakío*), who are able to dispense directly some drugs and medicines only available on prescription in other countries.

Photography

The light and colours make Greece a magnificent country for amateur photographers. The light in summer is usually stronger than it seems and can ruin pictures. Museums charge a fee for taking pictures (no charge at archaeological sites). Varieties of films (instamatic or 35mm) are sold on many islands, but are more expensive than at home. Do not take pictures on airfields (most of which are both civil and military) or of radar installations. Plane-spotters are totally misunderstood, too.

Place-names

You will find words in Roman script spelt several different ways. Twice the Greek Government has issued official spellings but almost no-one has taken much notice. There are also alternative spellings and names to many islands. Notable are Zante (officially Zákynthos), and Lésvos (officially Mytilíni). The official name is in timetables. For islands and places we have tried to follow those names and spellings used by British and American tour operators and airlines, but these vary, too. You may well find it useful to learn at least the letters of the Greek alphabet, so that you can recognise place names on maps.

Police

Greek Tourist Police (usually in an office in the police station) are helpful. You can tell them from other policemen by a flag on their pockets showing which languages they speak.

Alas, they are growing scarcer. The harshness or flexibility with which the Greek police apply the law can vary from island to island. You *can* be arrested for nude bathing or sunbathing. You *will* be arrested for getting involved in a brawl, drunken fight or for offensive behaviour. If you carry drugs you will be in *real* trouble. You could get life imprisonment for passing round a 'joint'. You will get one to three years at least for possessing even a small amount of cannabis, and Greek jails, they say, are not to be recommended.

Post

Signs of post offices (*tachidromio)* and post boxes are conveniently painted bright yellow. In small places, mail is not delivered to houses, but to a village centre – bakery, café, shop. Stamps can be bought at post offices or kiosks – *periptera* (small tax). Overseas mail is sent airmail.

The face of a monk from St John the Divine Monastery on Pátmos

Telephone and telegraph offices are separate from post offices.

Religion

Most Greeks belong to the Eastern Orthodox Church; there are some Catholics, especially on isles that were formerly Italian. Even those who are not seemingly religious regard the church with great respect. During the Turkish occupation, it was the symbol and rallying point for Greek culture and language and for freedom.

Siesta

Legally, all noise, including riding motorcycles and scooters, is prohibited between 14.00 and 17.00hrs in towns and villages, and after 23.00hrs in built-up areas. The afternoon can be a good time for looking around, but the heat can be fierce so *do* take a sun hat. Tavernas and cafés mostly stay open.

DIRECTORY

Student and Youth Travel

The best card to have is the International Student Identity Card (ISIC). If you are under 22 it can get you discounts on museums entrance, theatre tickets, archaeological sites and local travel. In the UK, under-26s may find cheap air fares through STA Travel (tel: 0171 361 6161), or USIT/Campus Travel (tel: 0171 730 3402).

Telephones

You can telephone or send telegrams from 'OTE' offices. Opening hours vary greatly. Overseas dialling codes are: Australia 00 61; Canada and USA 00 1; Ireland 00 353; UK 00 44 New Zealand 00 64; (then minus the initial '0' of the area code). Inland Service numbers: Directory Enquiries 131; Police 100; Medical Emergency 166; Fire 199; Roadside assistance 104; Telegrams-cables 165.

Time

Greek time is Eastern European, 2 hours ahead of Greenwich Mean Time.

Tipping

Not so widespread as in some countries. In high-class restaurants it is 10 per cent, but in tavernas or little restaurants small loose change suffices.

Toilets

Not the Greeks' strong point, even in little pensions. Public toilets are rare on the islands. It is best to order a drink or coffee in a taverna and use their toilet. Even that is liable to be primitive.

Tourist Offices

Greek National Offices:
Great Britain: 4 Conduit Street, London W1R 0DJ (tel: 0171 734 5997).
USA: Olympic Tower, 645 Fifth Avenue, 5th Floor, New York , NY 10022 (tel: 212/421 5777); Nat. Bank of Greece Building, Suite 600, 168 N. Michigan Avenue, Chicago, Illinois 60601 (tel: 312/782 1084); 611 West Sixth Street, Suite 2198, Los Angeles, California 90017 (tel: 213/626 6696).
Australia and New Zealand: 51–7 Pitt Street, Sydney, NSW 2000 (tel: 02-2411 663/4).
Canada: 1300 Bay Street, Main Level, Toronto, Ontario (tel: 416/968 2220); 1233 rue de la Montagne, Suite 101, Montreal, Quebec (tel: 514/871 1535).
Greece: **Athens**: 2 Amerikis Street, Athens 10564 (tel: 01-3223111).
Port of Piréas: Directorate of Tourism of East Mainland Greece and the Islands, Marina Zeas, 18504 (tel: 01-4135716).
On islands: Big islands with EOT offices include:-
Kós – Akti Koundouriotou Street, Kós Town (tel: 0242-28724).
Kefalloniá – Argostóli (tel: 0671-22248/24466).
For other islands, see text for **Tourist Office** and **Tourist Police** telephone numbers.

Travel Agencies

On larger isles there are private travel agencies, usually in fierce competition. Useful for booking ferry and air tickets but they will not help you with ferry companies they do not represent. Be especially wary in Piréas as they will tell you that there is no ferry to an island on a certain day as it is run by a company they do *not* represent.

LANGUAGE

Unless you know the Greek
script, a vocabulary is not of
very much use to the visitor. But
it is helpful to know the
alphabet, so that you can find
your way around; and the
following few basic words and
phrases will help too. (See also
Food and Drink chapter, page
108).

Alphabet

Alpha	Αα	short a, as in hat
Beta	Ββ	v sound
Gamma	Γγ	guttural g sound
Delta	Δδ	hard th, as in father
Epsilon	Εε	short e
Zita	Ζζ	z sound
Eta	Ηη	long e, as in feet
Theta	Θθ	soft th, as in think
Iota	Ιι	short i, as in hit
Kappa	Κκ	k sound
Lambda	Λλ	l sound
Mu	Μμ	m sound
Nu	Νν	n sound
Xi	Ξξ	x or ks sound
Omicron	Οο	short o, as in pot
Pi	Ππ	p sound
Rho	Ρρ	r sound
Sigma	Σσ	s sound
Taf	Ττ	t sound
Ipsilon	Υυ	another ee sound, or y as in funny
Phi	Φφ	f sound
Chi	Χχ	guttural ch, as in loch
Psi	Ψψ	ps, as in chops
Omega	Ωω	long o, as in bone

Numbers

1	éna	14	dekatéssera
2	dío	15	dekapénde
3	tria	16	dekaéxi
4	téssera	17	dekaeptá
5	pénde	18	dekaokto
6	éxi	19	dekaennía
7	eptá	20	ikosi
8	októ	30	triánda
9	ennía	40	saránda
10	déka	50	penínda
11	éndeka	100	ekató
12	dódeka	101	ekaton éna
13	dekatría	1000	chília

*As in all holiday destinations, tourist
and souvenir shops abound; this
one is on Mýkonos*

LANGUAGE

Basic Vocabulary

good morning	kaliméra
good evening	kalispéra
goodnight	kaliníkta
goodbye	chérete
hello	yásou
thank you	efcharistó
please/you are welcome	parakaló
yes	ne
no	óchi
where is ...?	poo íne?
how much is ...?	póso káni?
I would like	tha íthela
do you speak English?	milate angliká?
I don't speak Greek	then miló helliniká

Places

street	ódos
avenue	léofóros
square	platía
restaurant	estiatório
hotel	xenodochío

room	domátio
post office	tachithromío
letter	grámma
stamps	grámmatóssima
police	astinomía
customs	teloniakos
passport	diavatirion
pharmacy	farmakío
doctor	iatrós
dentist	odontiatros
entrance	ísothos
exit	éxothos
bank	trápeza
church	eklisía
hospital	nosokomío
café	kafeneíon

Travelling

car	aftokínito
bus	leoforio
train	tréno
boat	karávi

Traditionally male-dominated, the **kafeneíon** *is a place where Greeks can linger for hours*

Served in a variety of ways, octopus is an island delicacy on Aígina

train station	stathmos
bus station	stasi ton leoforio
airport	aerodromio
ticket	isitirio

Food

food	fagitó
bread	psomi
water	neró
wine	krasí
beer	bira
coffee	kafé

Fish

lobster	astakós
squid	kalamarákia
octopus	oktapóthi
red mullet	barboúnia
whitebait	maríthes
sea bream	sinagritha

Meat/poultry

lamb	arnáki
meat on a skewer	souvlákia
chicken	kotópoulo
meat balls	kefthedes
liver	skóti

Vegetables

spinach	spanáki
courgette	kolokithia
beans	fasolia

Salads and Starters

olives	eliés
yoghurt and cucumber dip	tzatsiki
tomato and cucumber salad	angouri domata
stuffed vine leaves	dolmades
'Greek' salad with cheese	horiatiki

Desserts

honeycake	baklavá
honey puffs	loukoumádes
semolina cake	halvá
ice cream	pagotó
yoghurt	yiaourti
custard tart	bougatsa

INDEX

ACKNOWLEDGEMENTS

Acknowledgements
The Automobile Association wishes to thank the following photographers
and libraries for their assistance in the preparation of this book:

AA PHOTO LIBRARY 72 Sými (S L Day), 82 Kokkári, Sámos (A Sattin),
124 *Kafeneíon*, Mílos (T Harris), 125 Grilled octopus, Aígina (P Wilson).

J ALLAN CASH PHOTOLIBRARY 23 Tíios Town, 30 Pottery, Sífnos, 35 Church
at Pláka, 52 Akrotíri, 58/9 White Rocks Hotel, 62 Ásos Bay, 65 Fruit Market,
67 Vrontis Bay, 113 Men at Tavern, 121 Monk, 123 Gift Shop.

INTERNATIONAL PHOTOBANK 11 Temple at Aphaia, 13 Aígina,
77 Kálymnos.

NATURE PHOTOGRAPHERS LTD 97 Gull (T Ennis), 98 Hawkmoth,
101 Wheatear (K Carlson), 99 Whip Snake, 105 Bee Orchid (P Sterry), 102 Fir
Tree, 104 Turtle (J Sutherland).

PICTURES COLOUR LIBRARY LTD 47 Mylopótamos beach, Íos.

SPECTRUM COLOUR LIBRARY 15 Póros, 17 Ýdra, 18 Fishermen, 20 Spétses,
25 Mýkonos, 29 Church at Sífnos, 41 Lunch, 43 Antíparos, 45 Náxos Town,
50/1 Kamári Beach, 53 Vineyards, 55 Shoe Repairer, 56 Defni Bay, 61 Sámi,
70/1 Ólympos, 79 Pátmos, 82 Kokkári, 87 Mending Nets, 94 Rigo Beach,
96 Skópelos, 107 Worry Beads, 108 Pátmos, 110 Melons.

ZEFA PICTURES LTD Cover Church on Páros, 4 Skópelos Harbour,
8 Skíathos, 9 Thíra, 10 Skópelos, 26 Windmill, 32 Sérifos, 37 Livádi Harbour,
49 Santoríni, 75 Kós, 84 Chíos, 88/9 Lésvos, 90 Límnos, 114 Mílos, 117 Ýdra,
118 Zákynthos.

Contributors for this revision:
Verifier: Robin Gauldie; Copy editor: Audrey Horne
Thanks also to the **Automobile and Touring Club of Greece (ELPA)** for
their assistance in updating the Directory section for this revised edition.